Disconnect Your Oughta Pilot

Spend Your Lives Chasing Dreams or

Disconnect Your Ought Pilots and Live Them

DeBorah Beatty

Disconnect Your Oughta Pilot

ISBN - 13: 978-0615664804
ISBN – 10: 0615664806

DeBorah Beatty
Created Life Strategies
Salem, OR

http://www.createdlife.com

contact@createdlife.com

Printed in the United States of America. Published by Created Life
Publishing. All rights reserved.

For bulk orders contact

editor@createdlife.com

DEDICATION

This book is dedicated to all of you who feel alone and out of juice. My intention is that this work will give you a kickstart to move from surviving to thriving and create a life you love in a manner that empowers you and thrills you every day.

CONTENTS

ACKNOWLEDGMENTS

I could not have gotten this written without the support and patience of my beloved husband, Rich, my good friends and editors, John, Sue and Kate and all of you who are going to put these words to good use in living your own dreams.

"Spend Your Life Chasing

Dreams or Disconnect Your

Oughta Pilots and Live Them!"

Hello! Your dream is calling you!

If you've spent years making other people's dreams come true at the expense of your own...

If those people you gave everything to and for have now moved on to live their own lives leaving you with only a sense of emptiness...

If you feel like you've given your whole life to make someone else happy regardless of what your heart was telling you...

And you feel resentment, aggravation, frustration and a feeling that you'll never be able to breathe freely again...

I have one question for you.

Have you had enough?

Thinking about all of you that I know who have shared how unhappy you are with their lives; how frustrated and angry you are that you've put everyone else's needs ahead of your own for so many years and now are left with nothing. You are smart, passionate, powerful women with a lot still to offer from formal education and life experience who are such treasures to those who know and love you.

And yet, you're suffering, you're feeling lost. I know how that feels. I've met so many people, primarily women, who have had to put their dreams aside to raise families, complete a task someone else gave them, or even work a really lousy j.o.b. just to make money to survive. This causes resentment, aggravation, frustration and a feeling that you'll never be able to breathe freely; not to mention a feeling of having been taken advantage of in a really big way.

I've been there myself, more times than I wanted to be. I was a single mother with responsibilities for 18 years. Dream? What dream?

I thought I needed the security of an 8-5 with benefits because I had someone else depending on it besides me. Nevertheless, through all the years in Corporate America, playing it safe, there was emptiness, a feeling that there must be something more I could do.

I couldn't make my expenses on a secretary's pay, so there was always at least one direct sales job on the side I could devote my entrepreneurial skills to. I sold Tupperware, Dynique Cosmetics, Herbalife and Latasia Jewelry, to name a few. I lived for the day when I could leave the corporate world behind and just do my own thing. I saw just how ridiculous and wasteful the processes for running the businesses were, and I was sure I could do better.

Other people took the pearls of wisdom I was sharing oh so freely and were doing well. I was offering tips and tricks for others to succeed and I couldn't get myself out of the cube farms! I got so burned out I changed careers and went back to school to become a Respiratory Therapist. Life was exciting for a little while. Working in Labor and Delivery taught me just how precious and how fragile life can be. The trauma team and heart team taught me what's possible for humans to withstand and rebound from. I spent four years learning until I fell one night in the ICU, sustained a career-ending back injury and was back to the "now what" question as I was faced with re-inventing myself yet again.

I didn't want to go back into administrative work. I'd had enough. I had a partial settlement from the back injury so took the opportunity to create DES Communications, a graphic design firm that was part of The ICON Group in Modesto, California.

Life was okay, not fantastic or mindblowing, but acceptable. I was managing. I had a decent relationship, a good business that was beginning to make a profit and a nice apartment.

Then the bottom fell out.

Again.

The phone rang. It was my mother asking if I could come and help her. She needed a hip replacement and needed me to stay with her. Still hoping for some sort of resolution to lifelong conflict and a long history of emotional abuse, I went. After all, I was an adult now and could take the higher ground.

My mother had always had issues – with my weight, with my outlook on life, seemingly with my taking up space on the planet.. I showed up, the dutiful daughter once again, only to find that in addition to a bad hip, she had metastatic cancer. She was still my mother, after all, so I agreed to help her out; putting my desires and visions aside to do what I "ought to" do.

One thing led to another and as days turned into months, I had to let things go – my home, my business (there was no online internet business available then).

Even my 8-year "perfect" relationship fell apart. He told me on the phone he'd found someone else and didn't feel like waiting for me to come home.

I found myself shouldering the weight alone.

My mother's cancer got worse and worse until she lost the ability to take care of her daily affairs. I felt forced to assume the financial burden of the household, and there went my limited savings.

My mother surrendered to brain cancer in June 1997. Losing a mother is hard enough, but with her passing, I lost my identity as well as my future.

All my life I'd been told things were done so I'd be "taken care of in my later years". When I was 7 my parents purchased property in Guam supposedly for me and my future. From an early age I was involved in property taxes, told about all the negotiations, plans and issues because "one day I'd have to know all this when it was my own responsibility".

I was an only child of loving parents and I had never had any reason to doubt I would inherit everything to make my "later years" comfortable. If I could just hang in there till that magical day, I could follow my own dreams and everything would be perfect.

It didn't work that way.

For some reason known only to her, my mother wrote me out of her will and left everything in trust for my daughter. I was left with nothing but the shirt on my back. Literally. The life of freedom I had dreamed of, planned for and expected was gone in the space of a breath. The years of waiting till I could take control of my destiny and pursue my own dreams were all for naught.

The executor of her estate showed up after my mother died to give me the news. I could not see the will, but it decreed that only my daughter could live in my mother's house now. I had to vacate the premises immediately and take only what I could prove I had brought with me when I moved in 6 months before.

I walked out of the only home I'd known for 22 years with one pair of pants, two shirts and $20. I had no family, no job, no money, no car, no friends (so I thought) and no home.

Living on the streets when you've come from a sheltered upbringing is a major education, I can tell you. There are a lot more demons out there to confront than gangbangers, weirdos and muggers. Most of them live within your own mind.

And yet, as time goes on, I'm increasingly grateful. It was during this time I began to discover what I was made of – my strengths, my weaknesses, my fears and just how far I was willing to go to survive.

I now choose to believe that my mother knew, on some level, I'd land on my feet. She'd had faith in me in spite of herself.

At first, the shock of everything hit me and I couldn't do much more than sit and cry. There were no shelter beds available, I was too ashamed to call anyone who might have a couch or spare room. I think I went a little crazy during that time. Just as I talk about later, I could have asked for help, but felt I had to battle on alone.

I gradually pulled myself together, I found a dry, warmish spot out of the view of the local constabulary to sleep and a park bench in the sunshine to sit and ponder life upon. Someone had told me where to get a hot meal and a shower and I was doing okay.

Sitting on "my" park bench two weeks later, I started taking inventory of my skills, my abilities and what I felt I could offer.

In the space of a breath, I was nobody's daughter, nobody's mother (my daughter had also taken off to parts unknown), had no expectations to live up to and an incredible freedom to just be myself for the first time in my life. The roles that had defined my identity no longer applied and I had no idea what to do with what I had. As the days go on, I thank my mother for giving me such a gift.

I'd always said if I only had the freedom to be what I wanted, I'd be happy. I'd gotten my wish. Oh happy day.

Who I am today and what I offer through my programs came directly out of that experience. I call myself a dream coach, not because I interpret your sleeping dreams; more so, I give myself that title (as well as several others) because what I do best is to ferret out that dream you've put aside for "Someday" and bring it into the light once more. We all have those secret dreams we've stuffed down in our mental closets deep into the dark recesses behind the coats and sweaters, waiting for someday when the time is right and we're free to follow our vision and live a created life.

What exactly is a "created life", you ask? A "created life" is one of your own choosing, where you make the rules and you have control. A created life is one in which there is no tomorrow nor is there a yesterday; there is only now.

When I say I live a created life, what does that mean, exactly? I have people ask me all the time if it's a spiritual/religious thing.

You know, it's just like many things we choose for ourselves — there always seems to be an explanation needed whenever you color outside the lines.

Here is the ultimate definition for you to use and integrate into your own chosen path:

A created life is one of your own making, however that looks at the moment; where you are living in the present moment and celebrating that whatever is happening, it is perfect and was caused by what you have done to make it so.

A created life, as I define it, does not get into theology, but it is deeply spiritual. I personally believe that within each of us is a spark of the Creator that imbues us with the power to make our own decisions and walk our own paths. When we give up control, become un-Conscious and start living on Oughta Pilot we become numb, our passion, our joy and our zest for being alive gets buried and stuffed down deep but the pain of ignoring our destiny begins to fester where it does the most harm. We try to ignore it, and sometimes we get really really good at pretending we're not here for a purpose we're not expressing. We wait for "someday" for the pain to stop but until we bring our Self back out into the light of day and let it breathe; it just seems to get worse.

Well, guess what. Someday is right here, right now.

Hello! Your dream is calling you! It's time to drag it out, dust it off and see what is in that package for you to explore.

Many of us have gotten to "a certain age" and are re-examining who we believe ourselves to be. Our children, if we had them, have grown and left the nest. We're either at retirement age or, with the current economic silliness, have been laid off after years on the job. We're asking ourselves, "now what?" and looking at our options. This is the time we're trying new things, creating our futures and pulling our dreams out of storage.

My Disconnect Your Oughta Pilot® program is designed to help you with reclaiming what you've forgotten or been lulled into believing you can't have.

11

What is an Oughta Pilot?

Living on Oughta Pilot is letting an "ought to" or a "should" be the primary motivation for how you live your life, the choices and decisions you make and the attitudes and feelings that arise.

"Oughta Pilot" is a term I have coined for living your life by someone else's rules, for surrendering your personal power and setting aside your own dreams and desires. In effect, you live your days trying to live up to what you have been told you "ought to" do.

Remember when you were a child and dreamed of being a (insert your dream here)? What happened to that? Did you do it? Or did a parent, teacher, coach or significant other talk you into putting that dream away and going for something more financially feasible?

In my case, I wanted to be a clothing designer and a musician. My mother thought that was too "out there" and carefully "guided" me into going to college to become a dental hygienist. I was out of my depth with all the left brain requirements and struggled and stressed through three years of attempts to get into dental school, without success. But I kept trying because I wanted to be a good girl and do what my parents expected of me.

At the same time, I was taking genetics, quantitative analysis, organic and inorganic chemistry, and other required prerequisites, I was also taking linguistics, psychology, sociology, economics, cultural anthropology and classes I found fun as electives. At the end of my third year, I had exactly the number of credits in my electives as I had in my major so, once it was clear I was a disappointment yet again and would "never amount to anything" anyway (according to my mother), I swapped and graduated a much happier person, although still a "failure", with a BA in Behavioral Sciences.

You see college "ought to" have been for a reason. It "ought to have" provided me with a career, it "ought to have" paid off.I was the first in my family to go to college and "should have made it count for something" but as it was, the whole "opportunity" was "wasted" on someone like me.

I wanted to pursue a career in the foreign services. I spoke three languages, had been raised on semi-foreign soil so why not? I had an aptitude for it and found the idea intriguing.

However, I graduated at the time of Watergate when nobody was hiring. Yes, Murphy loved me.

So, to pass time and earn a living, again following what I oughta do, I went to one of the oldest secretarial schools on the West Coast and once through that, took a job as a secretary which led to many years on cruise control, just doing what I had to do to exist. In the meantime I also married the first time (bad mistake) and had my daughter adding even more responsibility to others at my expense.

Can you relate? Have you ever been so caught up in doing what you think you *ought* to do that you put aside your dreams and slowly forget what you wanted to do? And soon, what you want to do is buried and lost?

5 Questions to Identify Your Oughta Pilot

1)   Do you spend your days working to live up to someone else's expectations?

2)   What would you do every day if you had no ties, limits, or responsibilities to others?

3)   What would you do if everything you were doing on a daily basis were to stop?

4)   What would you do if you knew you had 6 weeks left to live?

5)   How would you feel if you could do, be or have anything you wanted?

I've devoted the rest of my life to being a stand for your right to live at choice, doing what you were born to do, not necessarily what you have learned to do.

Are you spending more hours than ever going through the motions instead of living a joyous, created life?

Can you still remember what it felt like when you first began your journey?

Do you still hop out of bed, excited to face each new day? No? What has happened to change that? How can we reset the scene so we can have fun again, be excited again and find the energy we had to create our vision?

By the time you finish this book, you'll have a plan, several options and perhaps even a few solutions.

I suggest you read the following chapters with a notepad or journal as there will be exercises for you to do that you will want to revisit on occasion.

PART I: Look me in the eye...

Are you in there?

Living on Oughta Pilot

Where did you disappear to? Do you feel as if you're stuck on a carousel or a Ferris wheel that lost its brakes and won't stop? Are you always in a hurry to get somewhere but the destination keeps changing?

Do you just feel invisible? Is your life/business running you instead of the other way around?

These are the questions we need to ask ourselves. We're always so sure of where we're going and what we'll find there, but as the days go on and we begin to work towards the goals we've set for ourselves, the road gets dusty and the horizon always is just beyond our reach.

After a while, we get thirsty and sidetracked in all that dust so we lose focus. Once we've lost that, it's rather like being on the inside of a hamster wheel.

Are you doing what others say you "oughta" do? Or are you doing what your own heart and gut tell you to do?

We're born knowing what we're here to do. I call it our Original Song; the one we're born to sing. Somewhere along the way, we lose track of that and start singing someone else's melody. When we do that, our Original Song fades into silence and sometimes we forget to listen for it. There's a lot more about this further on, so keep reading.

Stop living the life others want you to live. Often we are so coerced into living our parents' missed opportunities and unrealized ambitions that we've been brainwashed into believing are our own. Follow your OWN path. Write down YOUR goals. Studies have revealed that people who write down their goals are five times more likely to achieve them.

When would you like to start a new career? Go back to school? Leave your job? How much money would you like to have saved? Set goals, and work backwards to achieve them.

Sing It Loud. Sing It Proud!

We are all born as musical entities. Some of the first communication between parent and child is in the form of a melody. For some cultures the music is more a part of who they are than others:

When a woman of a certain African tribe knows she is pregnant, goes to the jungle with other women, and together they pray and meditate until you get to "The song of the child."

When a child is born, the community gets together and they sing their song. Thus, when the child begins his education, people get together and he sings his song. When you become an adult, they get together again and sing. When it comes to your wedding, the person hears his song.

Finally, when your soul is going from this world, family and friends are approaching and, like his birth, sing their song to accompany it in the "journey".

In this African tribe, there is another occasion when men sing the song. If at some point the person commits a crime or aberrant social act, take you to the center of town and the people of the community form a circle around her. Then they sing "your song."

The tribe recognizes that the correction for antisocial behavior is not punishment; it is the love and memory of his true identity. When we recognize our own song, since we have no desire or need to hurt anyone.

Your friends know "your song". And sing when you forget it. Those who love you can not be fooled by mistakes you have committed, or dark images you show to others. They remember your beauty as you feel ugly, your total when you're broke, your innocence when you feel guilty and your purpose when you're confused.

Tolba Phanem
African poet

In our American culture, the music is not always so clearly a part of our lives. Not to the extent of the example above, anyway. One memory keeps me enthralled, however. When I worked as a respiratory therapist, part of my job was assisting with problem deliveries. I was there for over 200 births!

Some were fine; nothing to write home about, but occasionally, the baby was in trouble and had to be put into a NICU or Natal Intensive Care Unit. The therapists on night shift (including me) used to fight to go to the NICU on our lunch hours to help hold the babies. There was a nurse who ran the NICU that I loved to pieces. She had spent over 20 years as a military nurse (yes, she was in Korea in a M*A*S*H* unit, was tough as nails when it came to dealing with all of us and the doctors, but hand her a problematic infant and she was all gooey and mush.

She told us that there were studies done that proved that babies at risk did better, got stronger and went home with their families sooner when they were held, rocked and sung to. So that's what we did. We held the tiny tykes, we rocked them and we sang to them. Anything was fine, any melody, any words, they didn't seem to care, but they did respond to the human voice and closeness and they did thrive.

We all have a personal DJ playing old scratched records with commentary that have the volume turned way up so we can still hear our Original Song under all the noise. But in straining to listen to it, we still hear and process the scratched and warped sounds, too.

A word here about your Original Song, each one of us has one. We were born with it. The lyrics and the cadence are the basic rhythm of who we are and who we become in our lifetime. No two songs are the same, although they can be similar. The phrase about marching to a different drummer is more profound than we think.

Just as with your favorite album that gets scratched because it's played so often, during the process of growing up, socializing and being human, a lot of noise is recorded and laid down over the master track on the record of your life. Sometimes there's harmony, sometimes it's just scratches and odd sounds. The problems arise when we listen to the noise instead of the master track. It's so easy to get lost in a counter rhythm which is actually someone else's song they want us to sing instead of doing it themselves.

Are you living on Oughta Pilot or are you truly following your own dream? Are you singing your own Original Song or a parent's, teacher's or friend's?

Sometimes we're distracted by a complete stranger's song that we resonate with. When we can't distinguish our own any longer, it's possible to mistake another's melody for our own and we dance happily to it for a while until one day we wake up and realize that there's just that "something" that's missing from it and we begin a new search.

And then, one day, we meet someone or hear someone who shows us how to polish that scratchy old record until the noise is not so distracting. It never really goes away, but once we can hear the first few notes of our Song once again, it's so much easier to hear the rest of it and ignore the scratches and the dust specks.

Are you ready to polish your record? I have some great stuff to minimize scratches and bring out the beautiful notes of your Songs.

What is your Original Song? Do you think you could still identify it if you hear it? Or are those old records that your personal DJ playing in your head all the time so scratched and warped that the original melody is completely obliterated?

You may think your song is gone, but I assure you it is not, Listen for it intently when you're faced with a choice. It's there. I promise you.

And if you think you've forgotten what it sounds like, let me sing a few bars for you to remind you sometime. I've been given the gift of hearing your Song.

Of course, it may not actually be a song, but what I call your Original Song is a metaphor for your life's path, It could be a particular melody if music is your dream, but yes, I can uncover what you were born to do and I do it with several tools I have developed as well as those I've found that are complementary. Take your Original Song and sing it loud and sing it strong until it's an anthem; a driving beat that speeds up your heart and moves you forward to your destiny.

Watch Your Mouth,
Your Subconscious Is Listening

1)   Do you ever say something and wonder why in the world you would say something like that? The Open Mouth Insert Foot technique.

2)   Do you ever leave a less than satisfying conversation and then think of the perfect rejoinder for something said an hour ago?

3)   Do you ever wonder why people don't appear to be listening to you when you ask for something?

4)   Who is that little voice in your ear, really?

Here's something else to ponder.

Whenever we're in a conversation, we speak at an average of 150 words per minute (more if you're from the East Coast). We process about 750 words a minute, so where do the other 600 words come from? Our inner dialog that never shuts up.

Living on Oughta Pilot™ is letting an "ought to" or a "should" be the primary motivation for how you live your life, the choices and decisions you make and the attitudes and feelings that arise.

If we only pay full attention to 15 – 20% of what we hear externally and have the other 80% going on subliminally, it's no wonder we get derailed occasionally since who knows what we're being advised from our inner voice.

Let me tell you something about your inner D.J. This is the little voice inside your head that is never there to tell you you've done something right. Have you ever noticed just how negative those thoughts are? With every triumph you celebrate, there is always a little whisper in the background telling you that you could have done something a little differently to achieve an even better result. Am I right?

There was a minister at one of the churches I've attended who used to call it your "neener neener machine". Fun, huh?

How do you talk to yourself when you're not listening? What do you say to get your attention?

Contrary to popular belief, there is nothing wrong in talking out loud to yourself; even in public. It's been said, however, it's when you begin to answer that you should have cause for concern. In fact, every minute of the day we engage in a continuous internal conversation or "self talk," which is ultimately reflected in our moods, attitudes, actions and habits.

By monitoring and exerting control over this inner dialog we can begin to effectively control every other part of our lives. Facing and overcoming daily difficulties and recovering from setbacks are knitted into the fabric of human experiences. Likewise, striving to reach our goals and stretching beyond our perceived limitations, stepping outside our comfort zones, is also part of what it is to be a human being. To a large extent, much of our ability to succeed comes from our outlook on life. Success in business, building strong personal relationships, and maintaining a healthy lifestyle all stem from having a sunny disposition. As I've heard it often said, "no one wants to be around a doggone, disillusioned crybaby." It all comes down to how you talk to yourself on a daily basis.

Tune in to your self talk

I am sure you've heard it said before, "it's not what happens to you but how you react to it." The way you react to any situation is a direct result of how you explain it to yourself. We must learn to listen to the things we are saying to ourselves and change the languages from negative to positive. Whenever I find myself sinking into a low mood I immediately begin to ask myself, "What was I saying to myself right before I started feeling this way?" I then change my self talk. It may sound trivial to you, but another tactic I use is to eliminate certain words from my vocabulary.

For example, I chose not to use the word "problem." A problem is something that is perplexing and burdensome. I prefer the word "challenge." A challenge, on the other hand, is a test. It arouses and stimulates, you rise to meet it and it makes you stronger. Given the same situation, the two words will elicit totally different emotional responses.

I have also endeavored to erradicate the word "help" as in helping others. In my personal lexicon, helping someone is doing something FOR them, not giving them a hand up or support to do it themselves. I prefer to use the word "assist". Helping someone learn a thing doesn't work. You can teach them or let them learn. You cannot do it for them.

Your thoughts build self esteem

Self esteem and confidence are the foundation for competency and high achievement. It is impossible to develop any skills without first thinking highly of yourself and your ability to acquire those skills. Start your day in front of the mirror repeating affirmations such as, "I can do it," "I like myself" or "I am the best." These affirmations will build your levels of self esteem and self confidence. At first you may feel strange saying them.

Because, over the years, your mind has been programmed to believe otherwise. You may not believe you are the best right now and could construe saying this affirmation as lying to yourself.

I prefer to look at affirmations as telling the truth in advance. Additionally, since we were all designed for success, any self talk that causes us to be anything less than our potential is an even bigger lie. Your mind can only hold one thought at a time. Constantly repeating these affirmations will eventually replace the negative programming buried in your subconscious. Remember it takes 21 days to make or break a habit, so be kind to yourself and be patient.

Your thoughts manifest your goals

Buddha reminds us that "What we are today comes from our thoughts of yesterday, and our present thoughts build our life of tomorrow: Our life is the creation of our mind." Consequently, we need to keep our thoughts on our future and our goals. We should be constantly thinking about the person we want to be. By focusing on our goals, we will be guided to actions that lead to their attainment. Even when things go wrong, our attitude will not be one of resignation but instead, one of understanding that the path to success is paved with peaks and valleys. There may be setbacks, to be sure, but with FOCUS, we can reach the goals we set for ourselves.

Difficulties will be seen as opportunities to get stronger. The more you keep your thoughts on your goals, the more likely they are to be realized. As Henry David Thoreau says, "Thought is the sculptor who can create the person you want to be."

High achieving individuals are generally more positive, optimistic and resilient. They exert control over the small voice in their mind and as a result attract the goals and dreams they have for themselves. You too will be just like them as soon as you start making note of what you say when you talk to yourself.

Are you saying what you think you are saying when you talk to yourself and others?

I love the quote from Richard Nixon that goes, "I know you believe you understand what you think I said, but I am not sure you realize that what you heard is not what I meant." How many times is that true of our conversations with ourselves. How do you converse with others? If you're present in the dialogs you have with friends, family and acquaintances, do you listen to what is said? Is it positive? Do you internalize it or just let it go on by?

How are you describing your day? When someone asks you how it's going do you tell them it's great or do you begin the list of gripes you have stocked up from running out of coffee that morning to your boss telling you to do something you disagree with?

When someone asks you what you do, or why you do something, do you take a moment to listen to your Song and respond from your heart or do you launch into the well-rehearsed monologue of deprecating complaints you've used for years?

Exercise 1: Mirror 1:
<u>Life Changing Procedure</u>

The eyes are the windows of the soul. So, to the person you are capable of becoming, each evening, just before you go to bed, stand in front of a mirror alone and in the first person, present tense, look yourself in the eye and repeat with passion and enthusiasm the paragraphs below. The goal is to say them without reading them. Practice as many times as it takes to begin believing them and feel them resonate. Repeat this process every morning and every evening from this day forward. Within one week you will notice remarkable changes in your life.

I, _____, am a compassionate, respectful encourager who is a considerate, generous, gentle, patient, caring, sensitive, personable, attentive, fun-loving person. I am a supportive, giving and forgiving, clean, kind, unselfish, affectionate, loving, family-oriented human being and I am a sincere and open-minded good listener and a good-finder who is trustworthy. These are the qualities which enable me to build good relationships with my associates, neighbors, mate and family.

I,_____, am good to myself, true to my vision, and unswerving in my quest to live a created life. I deserve it. I have sacrificed enough. I accept it and rejoice that I once again dance to my own Original Song.

I, _____, am through holding back. I am a magnificent human being, capable of miraculous action. I can move mountains when I want to. I have created miracles in the lives of others. Now it's my turn.

I, _____, have had enough of the waiting, the wishing and the hoping. My time is here, it is now and it is MINE.

Repeat the process the next morning and close by saying, "These are the qualities of the winner I was born to be and I will develop and use these qualities to achieve my worthy objectives. Today is a brand new day and it is mine to use in a marvelously productive way."

Shake Your Meaning Maker

Human beings are meaning making machines. We're just hard wired that way. When something happens to us or with us, we just HAVE to make it mean something and the meaning we give to occurrences is not only extremely personal, but here's a concept, it may not be true!

I'd like you to take a moment to think back over your life. I'd like you to find your Triumphs. These are events that *you* are proud of, *you* enjoyed doing and *you* feel you did well. Think of 4 or 5 of them. They can be anything at all. The victories can be small and quiet or big and noisy. You get to choose. They are only according to *your* perceptions here.

Did you notice that on the way to recalling the times you excelled, a lot of memories of times you thought you failed surfaced first? Interesting wiring in your mind, isn't it? So now, I want you to look at one of those less than triumphant memories. Find a time when you felt unhappy, unfulfilled, even trapped in a job or in a relationship. I know personally I can remember many of these while I was working my j.o.b.s. (You all know the definition of a j.o.b.? It's a position that keeps you just over broke.) Hold onto this situation.

Ok, now I want you to take a piece of paper and draw two large circles, In the left circle, write the words, WHO, WHAT, WHEN, and WHERE. Write a keyword or two that describes the event you have in mind but ONLY WHAT HAPPENED in the left circle. Just the facts – no adjectives allowed!

Example: Once when I was working as an executive assistant to one of the partners in a big accounting firm, my boss returned from a particularly nasty business trip where one of his flights had to land because of mechanical problems, causing him to miss a connection and so forth. He, of course, blamed me for the lousy trip and I just knew my morning session with him would be less than fun.

I expected him to whine and complain and dump all blame on me and he did not disappoint me. I walked out of our meeting ready to tell him what he could do with his job, his business and just exactly how to do it. I felt incompetent, worthless and totally inept. AND the fact that I felt this way, also made me feel angry.

So in the left circle I would write something like my boss' name, business trip, when it happened and San Jose, California. In the right hand circle, write the words HOW and WHY. I would write how I felt: "incompetent, worthless, angry, frustrated" and why I felt that way. Get the idea? The left circle is really just what happened and the right circle is your reaction and thoughts about the situation – the MEANING you add on to the facts.

Within your Meaning Making Machine, there is a double ended arrow connecting the two circles. This is because these two circles begin to get collapsed into one as they feed into each other until our concepts about life begin to determine our experience of life. And the bridge between the two is "because". We conclude something from one experience and that shapes our next experience. In the example above, I went into the meeting *already* expecting my boss (a man, by the way, I had huge respect for as an effective leader, a canny manager and just a great person overall) to dump on me and make me feel as if his bad trip was all my fault and that I had failed to hold up my end of the work agreement. When I looked at the whole situation I realized I *had* failed, but not to hold up my end of our partnership, I had failed to make things which were out of my control fall into line with his expectations. I could not have foreseen an engine on his plane malfunctioning any more than I could the sudden shower that greeted him in London when he got there (by the way, also my fault). Ever have something like that happen to you?

Here's another story: When I was four years old, I decided I was not satisfied with the service I was receiving as the child in the family. I remember very clearly, unpacking my doll clothes from the small wicker suitcase I kept them in and putting my favorite doll and a change of underwear in it instead. I marched out into the living room where my parents were sitting and announced that I was leaving home and running away.

My father slumped down behind his newspaper. (I know now as an adult he was trying not to laugh at the peewee with her hands on her hips so outraged and full of vinegar.) My mother didn't make a fuss as she got up and opened the door for me out into the yawning maw that was the dark evening outside where the monsters live. You would have thought she'd turn on the porch light, but no. She just held the door for me. I remember looking out into the dark and deciding that since I didn't want to get eaten by the monsters my first night out on my own, I'd wait till morning when it was light and turned on my heel and returned to my room with as much aplomb as my small curly topped body could muster.

For many many years I made that incident mean that my parents didn't love me enough to stop me from going out into the dark and getting eaten. If they did, they would have said something. I went to great lengths until I was in my late 30s to prove to myself and to everyone around that I was unlovable and unworthy. Horse feathers!

It wasn't until I had a daughter of my own who tossed a similar gauntlet at my feet that I understood that they had just been calling my bluff and that as parents, could not give in to my puerile demands for attention.

You have a memory of some event. Write it out, everything you can remember about it, as detailed as possible. Include your feelings and descriptions. Now, going back to the circles, in the left one, write just the bare facts without any description or adjectives. In the right circle, write all the feelings you had/have about the event.

I want you to notice just how much your concept or your meaning of the event has colored all the events that bore even a cursory similarity to the original one. Did you already know what was going to happen? Did the next time meet your expectations? If not, did the time after that? How would you have felt doing that same thing today, before the exercise? How do you feel now about it?

Now here's the big question – WHY DID YOU FEEL THE WAY YOU DID WHEN THE EVENTS MENTIONED ABOVE HAPPENED? Was there a story behind your feelings? Why do you feel the way you do when the experience pops up again?

Take each experience and look at it apart from anything else. Journal your results.

Good luck and remember this, just as you made those experiences mean one thing, you can make them mean whatever you want now that you know better. If you have made an experience mean that you are stupid, why not try making it mean that you are just more discerning in your choices. If, as I did, you make an experience mean you're unlovable, why not change that up, too?

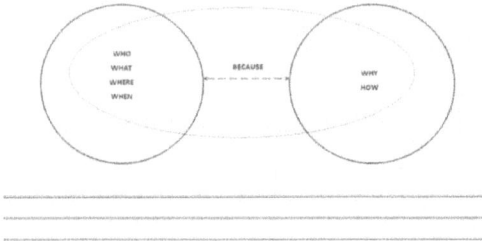

This is your opportunity to rewrite your life's story. It's really all a fairy tale. You made it up in the first place and now you have the privilege of writing it any way you choose!

Have a little fun with it. Remember you are the hero/heroine of the tale. It's all about you, this time, baby. So don't hold back. Let it flow.

The Joys of Failure

Here's the classic definition from the American Heritage®
Dictionary of the English Language, Fourth Edition
copyright ©2000 by Houghton Mifflin Company.

fail·ure   (flyr)   n.

1.   The condition or fact of not achieving the desired end
or ends: the failure of an experiment.

2.   One that fails: a failure at one's career.

3.   The condition or fact of being insufficient or falling
short: a crop failure.

4.   A cessation of proper functioning or performance: a
power failure.

5.   Nonperformance of what is requested or expected;
omission: failure to report a change of address.

6.   The act or fact of failing to pass a course, test, or
assignment.

7.   A decline in strength or effectiveness.

8.   The act or fact of becoming bankrupt or insolvent.

[Alteration of failer, default, from Anglo-Norman, from Old
French faillir, to fail; see fail.]

I realize that I am now and continue to be an amazing failure! *And I couldn't be happier.*

I am a failure at being what other people think I should be.

I am a failure at thinking the way other people think I should think.

I am a failure at looking the way other people think I should look.

Not being what other people think I should be has given me the freedom to explore my life and my opportunitites in different, innovative ways.

Not thinking the way other people think I should think has given me the freedom to explore self-education, alternative education and to have my education actually serve my needs.

Not looking the way other people think I should look as given me permission to be a unique individual with my own style and my own likes and dislikes.

Most of the dictionaries and 99% of society think of failure as a bad thing. I don't happen to share their opinion. How could you possibly succeed if you don't know how to fail? How do you recognize success when it happens if you don't have something to compare it to and recognize that it's different? We're always so certain we have failed when something doesn't work out but how do you know when it does if it doesn't a few times first?

So many of the people I talk with say they have a fear of failing, but I say they have a fear of succeeding. Especiallly if they've set themselves a big goal.

I have a neighbor upstairs who has a daughter who expects to do everything perfectly the first time. If she doesn't succeed, even if she's never even attempted it before, she says she doesn't like it and won't even give whatever it is a second chance. I think of all the things she's missing out on.

Look at Thomas Edison - he failed 10,000 times to make a light bulb. When asked how he felt about so many failures, he said "I have not failed, I have simply found 10,000 ways not to make a light bulb.".

Go try something you've never done before. Give yourself permission to fail. That way, you get a lot more joy when you succeed! After all, if you've never

 done it before, you have nothing to compare it to and you decide whether you've failed at all! Failure is all in YOUR mind. How many people do you know that blow off compliments saying that they could have done better and then list excuses? Especially when they've done something you are aching to just achieve a 10th of? It's all relative and it's all so very personal.

I give you permission (if you need it) to go try something new this next week. Something you've never done before and know nothing about. Go ahead, have fun.

George Bernard Shaw said it best when he said, "Life isn't about finding yourself. Life is about creating yourself."

Recycled Virgins

Have you ever wished for a do-over in your life? When I hear people sigh and say things like, "Oh, to be 18 again" or "I wish I was 30 again", I laugh. I would not want to go back and repeat any part of my life.

The way it is right now is perfect just as it is. I am the sum total of all my experiences and it gives me the wisdom to know there's more to life than the drama and moment to moment confusion that was such a part of my life back then. For me the past is just that – passed. I choose to live in the now, the present, and I look forward with expectation to what the next miracle I will create will be.

How would your life be as it is right now, if you knew and believed that you could start again at any moment, at any crossroads that faces you? What if I could show you a way you could wake up in the morning and create your day and actually have it go the way you plan?

No, you can't go back and literally reclaim your virginity. But let's take a look at what virginity is in the first place. Aside from the sexual connotation, the word "virgin" refers to unexplored, unexploited, chaste and untried. The word ignorance here is not an insult, but a statement of not having experienced a thing yet.

When we go through our lives on Oughta Pilot, we travel the same worn track over and over again. We do the same sorts of things over and over again while wishing we could do something new.

Quote: "Insanity is doing the same thing over and over again but expecting different results."

Most people will attribute this quote to Albert Einstein but there is no evidence to suggest that he made this statement. Whoever said it, however, was clearly inspired. It's true. And when we attribute the attempts to changing an element that is not working for us in our lives, when you do the same thing again and again and in the same way you will get the same unsuccessful, unsatisfying result.

The process here is to change something in the process and go at it again. Once something is different in the way you approach a thing, your outcome has to be different. But when you're paralyzed into repeating the same process because it's too scary to try something new, you'll find a way to create exactly the same result.

When you're scared and intimidated, close your eyes for a moment and breathe the end result in. Make it real. Smell it, see it, taste it, hear it, touch it. Whatever sense you need to use to make it real for yourself, use it then open your eyes and take the first step. Each step gets easier. It's the first one that's the doozy.

Exercise 2 – What's Past is Passed

Think of one experience you would like to change. How does it feel? What physical effects do you feel when you think of it? Take notice of those and write them down.

1.   If you could take that one experience and do it over again with a different result, what would it be?

2.   What would change, in your opinion, if you could?

3.   What would stay the same?

4.   Why do you think things would be different?

5. What would you have lost if you had not had the experience in the way you did?

Now think of something that happened that was one of the most amazing things you can remember. How does that make you feel? Can you feel the same emotions you did when it happened? Write down those feelings.

1.   What if you felt the way you do right now remembering the good experience when you think of the first one? Would that shift anything?

2.   Take the situation from the last question. Take one emotion, feeling or perception from the second situation and apply it to the first. What does that feel like?

3.   What does that do to the original memory?

4.   Do this with several other less than positive memories. What is happening to you physically right now as you do this? Detail it in your journal.

The Art of Falling On Your Face

Starting Over After You've Lost It All

Falling on your face is one way to know which end is up. When we were young and learning to walk, figuring out how to make those leg things work the way we wanted them to was always a challenge. The first thing we had to do was adjust to using them a different way. Once that part was more or less stable, we had to get used to the new altitude and changes in the way everything looked.

Our fields of view were not limited to ankles and the bottom side of the coffee table any longer. Now we were up above the edge and entranced by all the things on top of it.

We reached for something that caught our attention, and had to let go the desperate grasp we had on the edge of the couch for support and, wouldn't you know it, down we'd go, plop on our bottoms since we were still working on that elusive standing without help thing.

At first the sudden downward change in position scared us and made us cry, but when we figured out it wouldn't kill us, we tried it again and again till we got it accomplished to our satisfaction. Ok, standing was checked off our list. Now we needed to learn how to walk. Remember, walking is the art of falling forward and catching yourself over and over again before you can fall.

As adults, there's still a lot of that same thing going on. The process is basically the same only metaphoric this time. We're not trying to find our physical legs, we're trying to find our emotional, mental and spiritual legs. It's a well-known fact that we tend to chase new ideas and concepts and have all the focus of someone with severe ADD. Just about the time we think we're focusing all our energies on the pursuit of our chosen path, a bunny rabbit bounces across it and we just have to see where it goes. So, we let go of our support to chase it and wind up sitting down surprisingly fast and hard.

The difference is in how we react to perceived failure. When some people talk about losing everything, "everything" is very subjective. Especially lately, I've heard executives talking about having lost everything and meaning they've lost their job, and only have a few thousand in the bank. And I've known families sleeping in their cars who think they own the world.

For some, losing it all is realizing a minor disappointment, for others, the loss can be bigger.

When I talk about losing it all for the context of this book, I mean ALL OF IT; home, job, health, family, every last bit till all you have is what you were born with (and if you're lucky, the clothes on your back.) I've lost everything four times in my life and none of those times were through my own efforts.

Sh---tuff happens. The difference is in how you deal with it.

When you live a created life, you develop the art of falling on your face to a fine art. You become fearless in your willingness to risk everything and try anything if it will get you to where you want to go. If you make an attempt, and it is less than successful, you can regroup and try again knowing all you've lost is ignorance. Until you are WILLING to risk everything (with the emphasis on being WILLING) there's a level of holding back and playing it safe that gets in the way of your playing full out and getting out of the spectator section and down on the court and into the game.

I used to say to my daughter – Do something even if it's wrong. Sitting on the fence can get really uncomfortable.

Stages

The first stage you experience is shock and sadness. You just can't believe your life as you planned it is not going to happen. You have no foreseeable future, no options and no support. Or so you think. You need to sit with the grief and the raw emotion that happens if you want to overcome it. Be with it and experience it <u>all</u>. Then, let it go.

The second stage is assessing and reassessing what you do have to work with. Take inventory of what is at hand (no matter how little there is). In counting your blessings, you begin to see a glimmer of light. The last time I lost it all, my total physical assets were the clothes on my back, my driver's license, a toothbrush, a candy bar, $20 and a pen. That was all, but it was enough because I also had my experience, my knowledge, my innate strengths and skills. AND, I had rebuilt my life before, I could do it again.

The third stage is to make a plan using what you have. Figure out the immediate needs – shelter, food, hygiene – and start seeking a way to meet those needs on a basic level. Once those are handled, you have the space to work on the bigger plan. Take it a step at a time and you'll make it.

Following are 20 tips that will help you with planifesting (making a plan to manifest) your future. Find the ones that speak to you.

My 20 Planifesting Tips

1.   Say yes to your dreams

Say yes to your dreams and desires. You don't have to know at this moment what you will do or how you will do it. Simply acknowledge the inner voice that's been nudging you to do "something new".

Write "Yes! I accept my desires!" on a big piece of paper, put it somewhere you'll see it every day just to remind yourself that you are doing something. Start a journal. Use it daily to write down your ideas, goals, feelings and whatever is going on in your life.

I designed, sell and use a Gratitude Journal because I say everything that happens does so for a reason and some of the most difficult times have taught the best lessons.

You can purchase my journal from my website, or you can start with a regular notebook to see if you'll stick to using it. I guarantee that once you see the benefit, you will.

My journal is designed to do two things – create a living space for your dreams and engender consciousness of those that have come true.

When the things we've wished for have actually manifested, we forget we created those being in our lives until we lose them again and suffer the pain of loss. It's that human perversity thing again.

Using my Gratitudinous Attitude Daily Journal system, you recognize when an item moves from the left hand page to the right hand page and acknowledge that you've received it and are grateful for its being.

This is how it works:

On the right hand page is where you list what you are grateful for right here, right now; the things you currently possess. These are things like the food you have in your refrigerator, a job, a warm, dry place to sleep, family, etc. This is the count your blessings side.

Your page can be as lengthy and eloquent as you like or it can be just a quick list. It's your journal, you can do this your way. Remember, the more detailed you are, the more connected you will be. For those who prefer a graphic representation instead of a verbal one, I'll be bringing out a second edition without lines on the page, but in the mean time, you can use one of those spiral bound sketchbooks.

On the left hand page is where you list what it is you are intending to draw to yourself this day and the days in the future until it arrives.

The Universe loves to say yes to requests and here is where you make them. Remember also that It does not hear negatives. When you say you don't want to experience loss anymore or don't want to experience pain anymore, you'll get what you're focusing on; the loss and the pain. Do not detail what you do *not* want., Be clear, be detailed. and above all, be ready.

The language you use on this page is critical. Remember to always use the present tense and give thanks AS IF YOU'VE ALREADY RECEIVED whatever it is you're working on.

For example, you want a new home, a pretty little (or big) place that overlooks the water/mountains/meadow and makes your heart sing whenever you think of it.

On the left side of the page you would write something like, I am so very grateful for my new 3-bedroom house in (wherever). It gives me such joy to wake up there every morning and know it's mine. I walk to the kitchen, feeling the soft carpet under my feet and open the window over the sink that looks out over the creek behind the house let in the sunshine. I walk to the large side by side refrigerator and ….. (You get the idea).

Be clear, be detailed and above all, be ready!

The process actually becomes an effective way to get in touch with your dreams, visions and desires, make them more real and before you know it, they work their way from the left hand side of the page to the right.

Then, either using a binder clip or rubber band to keep the pages closed for at least two weeks, and preferably a month from the time you begin writing down your goals. Don't peek. This is truly the hardest part. Just be faithful to the task. At the end of a month or so, look back at where you started. I think you'll be surprised at how much progress you've actually made. Try it for yourselves and see.

Keeping a journal helps you get to know yourself better, and you'll see your progress when you look back. My journal has been especially helpful to me in those moments of uncertainty when I was feeling scared and could read about times when I felt confident or had faced something similar and made it through..

Even those challenges that I wrote pages about in my journal, when reading them later, seemed lighter, easier and sometimes even silly when I revisited them.

There's also no right way to keep the journal. What I've provided is a framework; a place to start. If you're more visual, doodle away, collage, be as crazy as you like. THIS IS YOUR JOURNAL. Have fun with it. Stretch yourself.

There is no right way to do this beyond keeping the two pages separate.

2. **Evaluate your beliefs.**

Grab a sheet of paper and write your beliefs about yourself, money, your business, and the future on the left hand side. Do it quickly, don't take time to think them through. Just write down as many as you can. Start the column with "I believe..."

When you've finished the list, read back over it. Are the beliefs listed what you thought you believed or are they different? See if they reflect what you want to believe. If not, write your edited beliefs on the right, and create affirmations you can repeat at least 10 times a day. Remember, these are YOUR beliefs. Anything on the list you've created and you can change them as easily as erasing them and writing something new. It takes 28 days to make or break a habit. Affirmations can help bring the change you desire.

Affirming our beliefs is a practice we all need to have. It puts the wheels of change and attraction in motion to allow the Universe to say yes to our requests.

It's so much easier to look forward when you can let go of whining and moping about the past.

One of the best affirmations I've ever used I got from a friend I met at an event four years ago. Gwynne Warner of Ten Thousand Blessings Feng Shui shared this one.

I'm sure you can use it as well: Her advice is to write in nine times for nine days in red ink.

> *"The tide of Destiny has turned and now everything comes my way."*

You may find that the beliefs you hold near and dear may actually have been someone else's you adopted somewhere along the line and you can let them go now if they don't work in favor of your own.

3.   Do what you love.

Discover and clarify what you want to do be and have. It's your life, you have a right to claim it and create it the way you want it to be.

As an entrepreneur, an artist, a business owner or even as a human being, if you don't know what you love to do, think back to what you loved to do as a child. What about that was it that you felt so strongly about? Can you still do it now? Do you still want to?.

When I was little, I loved to perform and entertain people. Now, I'm doing what I love again; giving seminars that make a difference in people's lives. I heard Kathie Lee Gifford on the Today Show a couple of weeks ago said she was told by her father to figure out something she loved and find a way to get paid for it. Sounds good to me, how about you?

Most of us know instinctively as children what we want to do/be when we grow up, but teachers and parents and well-wishing adults often talk us out of it if what we want to do doesn't fit with their reality. And being children, we're not often given the chance to disagree.

The opportunity to disagree with the path others have chosen for us usually surfaces when we become teenagers and are seeking our individual identities. Our Original Song is loudest then and we either choose to listen to it or dance to the rhythms of another we find more seductive. Pressure from our peers entice us to forsake what we want to be one of the cool kids, the group, the homogenous crowd.

Whatever we choose, we follow until it no longer serves us and we listen for our own melody again. It's always there, just sometimes it's covered in scratches or so soft we need to strain to hear it.

We need to lovingly polish our records, listen for what still works and discard what doesn't.

4.   Do one dream thing daily.

"Act As If" – How many times have you heard and discounted this phrase? It isn't always easy, I know. Be gentle with yourself and take small steps. Think of turning a cruise ship instead of a speedboat – tiny changes make a smooth turn. The Japanese have a tradition they call Kaizen, making small changes to create big ones.. Think of turning a cruise ship. You can't make a fast right turn; you need to make small corrections a few degrees at a time to stay afloat. Yet for every degree you change on the heading, you could wind up hundreds of miles away from where you were going.

If you change one thing, even if it's teeny tiny, every day, before long you'll be surprised at how it transforms your whole world.

Recently I spoke with Ani, who was upset that she had to go back to work instead of continuing to work on her business, which was just not getting off the ground. She felt like she was giving up the dream yet again and was devastated that in her midlife years after successful careers in big business, she couldn't make a go of her dream.

Together we worked through why she felt that way and ways she could still keep her dream alive. My friend Carrie Greene of www.carriethru.com talks about looking at getting a job to bring in more cash flow as getting a business loan for your business.

Looking at the job as being more of a business investment, it wasn't so difficult to accept. Ani began looking at the opportunities her new position would give her, insurance, regular income, and public contact. She set a plan to work for a year while doing all the back end work to get the business going – developing and creating product, new website, blog, social networking to create buzz, and more – and suddenly was actually looking forward to the whole experience.

Checking in with her not too long ago now that she's been there 6 months, she actually likes her job and may stay longer. She's getting a lot done on both sides now that her financial stress is mitigated.

5.   Be Afraid — Be Very Afraid!

Go out and scare yourself. Seriously. Are you afraid of doing something, saying something or going somewhere? Do it anyway! Take a buddy if you need to, but do it. What's the absolute worst thing that could happen if you do it? (Ps-s-st - you might just find you have something new to light up your life!)

My first night on the street after my mother died was the second worst night of my life. I was cold, hungry and in shock. I didn't know where I could go or what I needed to do to be safe when all I wanted to do was sleep and have everything just be a dream I could wake up from. I crawled under a hedge in the public park and cried. I had $20 that had to last until I could make more. I had no interview clothes, I had no way to get to an interview or type up a resume to submit even if there were jobs. Everything seemed so very overwhelming.

It was easier once the sun came up, but not much. Thank God it was June and the sun was shining to dry off the nightly dew that had soaked through my clothes. I knew I had to find a way to survive. I was good at surviving.

I'd come through typhoons blowing my home away, boyfriends using my rent money to buy drugs, evictions, knife fights in fourth grade growing up in Guam and if I could survive all those things, I could beat this.

The thing that got me through that day and the next few nights was the knowledge that I could and would survive, no matter what. I'd lost it all before and made it back. I could do it again. I was also present to the thought that I didn't like surviving; I was ready to thrive this time.

Being fearful of something and doing it anyway builds courage and confidence. One of my clients made up the maxim "I'm afraid, and?!" to help her take action and challenge herself to do things that scare her.

You probably won't go out and do whatever it is you dream of perfectly the first time out of the gate, either. If you think you will, you need to get over yourself or create better goals for yourself.

Give yourself permission to fail. You will, you know, but in failing, you'll learn which paths work and which don't. I always think of a baby learning to walk. Walking is actually the art of falling on your face, but catching yourself before you do. Babies fall a lot when learning to use those things called legs, but they pop back up and try again as soon as they're down. Especially if they have someone they trust telling them it's okay and cheering them on.

My friend Stephan Stavrakis says to go out and "suck a lot" in the beginning to get the bugs worked out. The only way you will acquire mastery is practice, practice, practice.

Fear is a good thing when what you're contemplating is dangerous or life threatening.

If what you're afraid of is bungee jumping or cliff diving, that's a different story, but in this context we're talking about something related to your life expression or trying something new in your business. It's just life, not brain surgery.

If you are planning on going bungee jumping or skydiving for your birthday, and you've taken all the steps to ensure your physical safety, I say go for that, too!

6.   Accept all your feelings.

Vulnerability, uncertainty, doubt, fear and insecurity are all normal feelings. None of us like feeling we are anyone's mercy, but they pass. Eventually those awkward fears get replaced with confidence, certainty, and faith in your own ability. Create a positive inner dialog with yourself, and talk about your feelings with a trusted friend. Remind yourself that you are perfect just the way you are, that you're safe and all is just as it's supposed to be. What you resist, persists. When you avoid feeling what you're feeling or dismiss your emotions as silly or useless, you prolong their effects.

One of the things that makes us human beings is our capacity for feeling. We need to honor all our feelings from the deep doldrums to high excitement.

Whatever you're feeling at any given moment, accept that feeling as honest and good and just sit with it. If it doesn't serve you, once acknowledged, it will fade away. If it does, put it to use.

Feelings are not good or bad, they just are. They exist for a reason, and only we can provide those reasons. And since humans are "reasonable" people, since we made up those reasons in the first place,, we can change them. Personally I prefer to be UN-reasonable and act out of choice.

Your Oughta Pilots live in the "becauses" of your life. If you can eliminate the reasons, you can eliminate the becauses and disconnect those shoulds and oughtas that no longer serve.

There is an exercise I do in my Disconnect Your Oughta Pilot™ Program called, "Shake Your Meaning Maker". It has to do with how we create meanings for everything and since we create them in the first place, we can change what experiences mean to us. In order to do that, however, we have to be clear on what the experiences were in the first place to integrate and discharge the emotional investment we've made in the stories that have evolved.

This is a very powerful process because in breaking down where we created meanings for our experiences in the past, we can see how we expect similar results if opportunities resembling them appear and thus miss taking full advantage.

As an example, Joe's first attempt at self-employment was selling widgets at a Saturday market when he was 12. His venture failed miserably and made a huge impression on his young entrepreneurial soul. His story was that prospective customers thought he was not able to sell widgets in a booth at a market. He resisted doing any sort of business that involved overt sales for years.

After we plugged in the facts, he could see that in fact, he'd been simply unprepared at that time to sell those widgets since he had no plan to keep the enterprise going. It had nothing do to with customers, and nothing to do with his ability to sell. Sometimes truth is there but hidden. Look at the picture below. Do you see both images?

7.   Finish unfinished business.

Make a list of things that niggle at you and that need to be completed, repaired or finalized. Make room for your new life by finishing the things on your list one by one. Make a list of the creditors you've been ignoring. Jot down the people you wish you had time to hang out with. Every day, take one thing on that list and get it completed, whatever that takes. If the task is a big one, see if there's a way to divide it up to make more of it do-able at one time. Time Management Professionals call this "chunking" and it's the preferred method of getting tasks accomplished instead of multi-tasking.

I had a friend, JoAnn, who was having a tough time with depression. Everywhere she turned, she had made promises that she was just too overwhelmed to keep. She felt awful, empty and powerless. We tried making the list as above with her. Every day, she either called one person she'd lost touch with and made contact. She made arrangements to take care of the things she had let slide and soon, she said she felt better, more confident.

She told me she didn't feel like she had to hide when she went out, or not answer the phone. She took back control of those things she could and began to see a professional who could help her get a grasp on the things she didn't feel she could.

JoAnn also had issues with managing her work/life balance. She felt like she was working all the time and never had a moment for herself. We created Sacred Time on her calendar when she could just do whatever SHE wanted to do at that time. She began scheduling in the time as if it were for a client and was much happier.

8.   Knowledge Is Power.

Take classes or attend seminars in person or online or read up on the necessary information to learn the nuts and bolts of something new. Find a mentor who has done what you want to do. Ask tons of questions and resurrect the "Information Interview".

An information interview is designed to get you just that: information. I learned the technique in the early 80's and used it mostly in employment searches. Find someone who is doing what you want to do and interview them to find out what they think about their job, what it consists of and what the requirements really are as opposed to what is on a job bid.

The way I like to do these interviews is to find someone who is competent and successful doing something I want to do. Then I schedule an interview to ask them all the questions I have. Information interviews are a wonderful way to get the real story and background on tasks. I've used them to gain insight before quoting a graphics design job (back when I did that), before quoting projects and in general, for my radio shows on BlogTalk Radio and Bitwire Media.

The interviews don't have to be formal. You can meet over coffee or tea for 15 or 20 minutes and find out what you want to know. Just make sure you have your questions ready and get to it. You never know where this will go, I've had several partnerships of excellence come out of these meetings since the other person gets to know you, too!

Another option is to get formal education about the task you're contemplating taking on. When I wanted to start doing textile design and my own line of clothing, the first thing I did was take a design class for textiles at a local community college. I had doubts when I walked in and found that most of the class were on their third time through, but once I relaxed and started playing, I had more fun than I ever expected while learning another new skill I could use to get closer to my dream. And yes, I wound up taking the class three times myself just for the fun of it! I actually found it freed up my artistic, right-brained side and made me more effective all around.

It may be something as simple as watching a YouTube tutorial, but the more you know, the more effective you are.

Don't hesitate to explore, you don't have to have a point to your queries.

When I was in high school, I wanted to write fan fiction (based on popular TV shows, movies or in those days book series) for Doc Savage. One of the characters was always cited for wanting to use 15-syllable words whenever a single one would do. I did not have the vocabulary to write for Johnny's dialog so one of my best resources was the massive library dictionary.

The old Oxford was dog-eared from years of young women fingering its pages. I can still hear the delicate whisper of the pages as they turned and smell the old book scent. I'd look up one word which led to another and another until I'd spend hours reading the dictionary and as a result of starting one quest, I'd discovered not only a love of writing, but a real talent for linguistics and etymology as well.

(Of course my love of words and how they're used in sentences to convey meaning has also fed my love of fracturing the English language for my own benefit, but that's another story).

9.   Accept and believe compliments.

When people offer compliments don't play modest or humble. Accept them, believe them, enjoy them; you've earned the credit. Every one of us hungers for acknowledgment when we do something. Why not accept it when it comes? If what you're being told tickles you to the marrow, let the person giving you the compliment see that you're enjoying what they say. I don't know where it started being a bad thing to acknowledge accomplishments. Just say thank you and breathe in the good stuff.

One of the exercises I love doing at my workshops is to call each person up on stage with me, introduce them to the audience and say a bit about who they are as a person and what they've accomplished. Then the audience applauds that person and they have to stand there and just breathe it all in. It's surprising how difficult it is for some and how life changing it is for others. There are almost always tears but that 2 minutes of acknowledgment is always one of the high points of the weekend.

10. Acknowledge your gifts.

Recognize and acknowledge your gifts and special talents. You are a unique child of the universe unlike any other. Acknowledge that you are a master at doing what you do the way you do it . No one can do what you do exactly the same way. Make a list of the things you know or you've been told you are excellent at. Come on, I know there are some.

Oh, wait, do I hear one or both of your parents and your teachers telling you to be humble and that acknowledging just how amazing you are is a bad thing? Tell 'em to kiss off!

This is where you can.

And while you're sitting in your sacred space with nobody else around, go deeply into yourself and write down those things you know you love to do, but no one else even knows you can do. Do you love to do puzzles? Sew clothes? Doodle or even paint? Do you write yet hide your work away so nobody can criticize? What are the things you wish others knew you know how to do? What would be one thing you could do to let them in on your secret?

I found it quite sad a few weeks ago that among the contestants for NBC's <u>The Voice</u> television show, there were several who said that their whole lives revolved around their music and their singing, but that it was a secret they had never shared. Nobody else even knew they could sing. (They do now, though!) They excelled at a number of other talents, but never discussed the one thing that they were really passionate about with their family or friends until the opportunity to audition for the show gave them an excuse, shocking and surprising the people who had known them and loved them for years!

I understand sometimes something is too precious to entrust to the opinions of others. But that's a story, too. We made that part up. Once you've shared something truly precious with someone you trust, it develops a life of its own growing, glowing and attracting more of itself until you have achieved your vision and are on to bigger and better things before you even realize it!

Exercise 3   Mirror 2

Find yourself a comfortable place to stand or sit where you can gaze for a period of time into a mirror.

Look at the person in the mirror: The person not the reflection. Look at them as if they were a different person. Look at their hair, their eyes, their brow. Think about the following questions:

Is this person someone I can trust?

Does he/she look like they know what they're doing?

Do they look confident or scared?

Can I admire this person?

Could I love this person?

What do you feel when you look at that person? Is it simple vanity (hair out of place, need more color, etc.) or is there something deeper?

Spend about 10 minutes with yourself. What discoveries are you making about the person in the mirror?

Now, go deeper. That person you just got to know is you. Does the reflection in the mirror represent the person you want the world to know as you? Or is there something missing? What is it, just notice it and write it down for later. This is not the time to spend on blame, excuses or getting something fixed. Just notice where the incongruities exist.

Look at your posture. Is it confident? Or tense? Frightened even? Hesitant? Make note.

1.

11.   Give up excuses.

If you hear yourself making excuses, write them down and become consciously aware of them. I have a client who stopped making them in favor of a simple, "I didn't get it done".

There's a phrase that I try to remember, "Could have, Would Have, Should Have... Didn't". It basically means that all the time and talking in the world about what you might have done in a different circumstance doesn't change the fact that you just didn't do it. Give up blaming, give up excuses. Just take a breath and start again.

Making excuses takes time and energy away from actually working on the project involved. How many times over the years have you had to listen to someone going on and on about why something didn't happen when they could have just tried again and possibly even have done it in that same space of time (or less). Don't you notice how much time it takes to figure out a reason something doesn't go the way you think it should? I prefer to back up and start again from a different direction.

Remember, watch your mouth, your subconscious is listening. Eliminate negativity. Become aware of when and why you say "I can't," and change it to an open-ended question like "How can I?"

12. Accept confusion.

Confusion is part of the process of starting over. It serves to make us take a second look at our options. Write about it in your journal, talk about it with friends, and know that it will pass. What we resist persists.

Know there is no "right" time or "right way" to do what you dream. All we have is 24 hours a day. Period. Just like everyone else.

It's what we do with that time that matters. If we expect clarity always, we're doomed to be sadly disappointed. That's why we're not here on this planet alone. We need others to help when we're confused.

13. Declare your choice.

Next time you're asked to do something, say yes or no based on what you really want to do. If you're undecided, say so.

People will respect your choice and your forthright answer. How many times have we agreed to do something against our better judgment, but didn't want to "rock the boat" and be the party-pooper?

Here's the secret (and I believe it must be a secret because very few seem to know this). *It is perfectly acceptable to decline a request.* Requests have three possible responses. They can be declined, accepted or modified. Feel free to pick one of the three the next time someone asks you to do something you're not real keen on. Don't worry that you'll offend the person making the request if you decline. They'll find someone else to do it or find a way to do it themselves.

14. Avoid self-judgment.

If you hear yourself saying things like "I'm stupid," or "I can't do that, I'm not smart enough", gently remind yourself that you have chosen to accept yourself as you are. Those judgments you make about yourself may not be how you feel about yourself at all, but may be simply echoes from other people. Terry Cole-Whitaker had a great book back in the late 70's called "What You Think of Me Is None of My Business." I recommend it.

I also believe that our personal judgment of ourselves comes from listening to other's perceptions and taking them to be true. However, those other perceptions are a result of their listening to external perceptions from those they trust and so on and so on until it's a generational, self-perpetuating, thought-to-be-true-ism.

Avoid judging others. It doesn't serve either of you.

I'm here to tell you, your frustrations can stop with you. Just be, and/or cause, but don't be just because.

15.   Expect resistance.

You can expect to feel resistance within yourself as well as from those around you whenever you want to attempt something out of the ordinary. Work through the "I don't wanna's" by acknowledging them and doing what you need to do anyway. You've spent however many years you've spent on this planet being told you can't. That's a big thick wall to break through, but you can do it. Just take a deep breath and put one foot in front of the other, figuratively or physically.

My friend Dana had been a coach and a professional speaker for 10 years. She was eloquent, effective and dynamic in her presentations. Still there was something that was missing for her, some way she didn't feel that she was truly connecting with her audience.

She started looking at all the places where she was not being authentic and sharing all of herself, no matter how badly she wanted to. It was a difficult task to be completely honest with herself.

One day she figured it out: the part she was withholding from her audiences was a deep secret she'd been carrying for many, many years. At least she thought it was a deep secret. She was overweight and secretly felt that if she dressed a certain way, or stood a certain way in front of her audience, nobody would know and it could be her own "dirty little secret".

She laughed when she realized how silly she'd been. Nobody in her audiences cared about what she looked like, and she couldn't definitely couldn't hide her voluptuous curves behind a microphone pole. *Of course* they could see she was overweight. Big deal. They were there for her message. Once she gave that fear of her "dirty little secret" being discovered, she could just relax and be herself in front of the room. Now, it didn't happen overnight. Her fear was extremely deep-seated and took being conscious of her choice to be free of it every minute she was on stage for awhile. Her effectiveness and her profits took off after that and she's much happier with herself now.

To this day, whenever I walk into a room full of strangers (and even not strangers) I feel anxiety. The old scratchy records start up, The loudest song that plays most of the time is"What If They Don't Like Me?". The difference is that I've learned to polish the record to hear through the scratches to where my Original Song is playing.

16.   Answer your "what if" questions.

What if it doesn't work out? What if you don't make any money? Use your journal to write down your what ifs, and answer them. For example, to answer "What if I don't make any money?" you may respond, "I can get a part-time job while building my business."

How well you answer the questions will show you how prepared you are for what you say you want to do. I was talking to a friend the other day about a choice I had to make. He asked me, "What's the worst that can happen to you if you choose either side of the equation". It hit me like a ton of bricks, he was right; all the wringing of hands and the perspiration of cogitation was just adding a layer of drama to the situation. No matter which side I chose, I wouldn't die, I wouldn't starve, and nothing much would change. Once I realized that, it was much easier to choose what I wanted to do without the "because" getting in the way.

Sometimes there is also a need to ask the age of the conversation you're having with yourself. Are you hesitant, afraid or reluctant to do a thing because the thing is too big? Or is the hesitation, fear and reluctance actually coming from an older, much younger conversation that may or may not have anything to do with what you see before you.

17. Practice patience.

There's a very old joke that goes, "How do you get to Carnegie Hall? – Practice, Practice. "

Patience is a muscle that needs to be developed and strengthened. The more you exercise it, the stronger it gets.

Next time you're in a traffic jam or waiting in a line, practice patience. Instead of getting irritated or upset at the people in front of you or a cashier trying to do their job, take a deep breath and count to 10. Be conscious of your desire to act and take the opportunity to control the urge.

Don't have the money you need to purchase something and no credit to float it? Save up for it. If it's meant to be, it will still be there when you can afford to purchase it. If not, perhaps you didn't need it after all.

Having trouble putting money aside in a savings account? Take 10% off everything that comes in. It may only be a couple of dollars, but if you put that away in a savings account or some other investment, in short order, you'll have a tidy sum saved up. There's always some discretionary income somewhere in your daily expenditures. Invest it instead of spending it on something that you don't really need and create a financially sound future.

I have a canning jar on my desk that I put loose change in. I call it my Bubble Jar. Do you know about bubbles? Bubbles are a creation that should not exist. They are so fragile and their walls are only a cell or two thick. If you breathe too hard on them they pop and go away. If the sun is too hot and the internal temperature of the bubble goes above a specific range it will burst. If you haven't gone outside with a jar of bubbles recently, run (don't walk) down to the closest dollar store and pick up a jar. Super cheap entertainment and with every bubble you create, send off a dream or a concern and you choose what it means when the buble burst. Take a break every now and again to get back in touch with the delicate fragility of bubbles. You'll be better for it.

Just like our dreams, they can disappear if we look at them too hard or if the sun shines too brightly on them. My bubble jar is for whatever I cannot see coming that I am working to draw to me. Serendipitous Savings. I've actually emptied it a few times over the past two years and put the funds into a savings account. It makes me smile every time I see it.

18.   Turn off your personal D.J.

I've seen clients miss opportunities when they turned down or did not pursue projects because they listened to their Personal D.J. playing old tapes that said they didn't have the right skills, the right brochure or the right product. They wanted to get it 100% perfect before they move forward. I'm here to tell you, you'll never get it 100% perfect *unless* you give it a go and fail a few times. Remember watch what you say, your subconscious is listening.

The next time you feel compelled to turn down an opportunity because you think you lack some skill or resource, figure out what would be necessary for you to grab it. Do the Meaning Maker exercise and see if you really don't already have what you need or if you're linking it to a previous experience.

19. Ask for help.

When you're most challenged and least likely to ask for help, reach out and ask. That's the time you need it most. I can attest to the power and clarity that comes from asking for help when we least want to ask for it.

After my mother died and I was on the streets, I could have asked friends if I could stay with them. I had several nearby and they were the kind of friends I could go to with anything.

Yet, because I was too close to the problem and totally overwhelmed with the enormity of what had happened, I put myself through three of the worst weeks of my life when it wasn't necessary. But I couldn't see a solution, couldn't rise above the challenge. Not then, anyway.

If you're overwhelmed and can't get your to-do list completed, find someone to help you; college interns, virtual assistants, even friends. There are a number of programs through many of the States to train people on unemployment in new careers. Look into those to see if you can offer your business as a training ground and get your tasks completed as a by-product.

Now, I have to share this with you. No matter how enlightened (I hate that word, but it works here) you think you are, every now and then, life comes up and smacks you between the eyes with a clue by four. I had that happen just this week. I'd like to share this with you because I know better than to fall into this particular trap. I know better and I walked straight into it.

Here's what happened. Since April 11, of this year I'd been dealing with a lot of life challenges. My husband had a total hip replacement (he's doing wonderfully, by the way) that was more involved than originally planned requiring him to spend an extra day in the hospital. That was Wednesday. Friday, we came home from the hospital and got him safely lying down from the extra exertion of walking all the way from the car to the apartment when I heard thundering up and down the stairs.

We live in a three story apartment building and every time the people upstairs hurry down the stairs it sounds like a herd of elephants has escaped the zoo. When I opened my front door to see what was going on, I was drenched in water. There was a fire in the top apartment that melted the pipes under the sink and water was pouring out of the apartment and down the stairs.

At the same time, water began pouring out from the ceiling fan in our dining room, the electrical outlets in the kitchen and the carpet was getting soppy. I grabbed towels, trashcans and buckets and started in trying to mop up the water before it got out of control.

Furniture needed to be moved. Cupboards had to be emptied. The carpets were torn up and those nasty, noisy blowers put in place for three days. I was scared Rich would trip and fall. Finally, when the carpets were deemed to be dry, we remembered that we had renters' insurance and called them.

To make a long story short, (I know, I know, too late) we were in temporary housing now for almost three weeks. I'd gone back to my j.o.b. and had been running myself ragged.

I'm a member of Women of Visionary Influence. It's a wonderful organization dedicated to building relationships and mentoring among women. I was supposed to attend our monthly meeting last Saturday and when the parking for the event was not the best, I lost it and told my chapter president I would just see her next month.

The next day I got a phone call asking me to join the Board of Directors of the chapter on a conference call. I had recently taken a position on the Board and I immediately went to, "they're going to ask me to step down and replace me."

What this group of amazing women wanted was to offer me their support and love; to ask what I needed and how they could help. I've never been so touched. It reminded me that the most important thing when feeling overwhelmed is to reach out and ASK FOR HELP. This is the trap I walked into with both eyes open. I was feeling helpless, powerless, just trying to make do and get through this mess. Frustrated, alone and feeling sorry for myself, I had sacrificed my own well being for the joys (?) of martyrdom.

The women of WOVI were offering their open arms and hearts for me to take what I needed to recharge my spirit and let me know I was not alone, not helpless and re-validated my self in the space of just a few minutes.

It's way too easy to fall back into past habits. I'd slid back into survival mode instead of living at choice as I coach my clients and tell everyone to. The difference is, this time I have friends who will remind me of who I've chosen to be and about the life I've chosen to live. I do hope that if you find the dreaded dark cloud hovering over you that the first thing you do is ask yourself who you can call to help.

This does not diminish your abilities.

You can do it all by yourself, you just don't have to do it alone.

And by the way, ou don't need to do it all by yourself; you don't need to do it all in the first place!

20. Trust your instincts.

Others may tell you that you're crazy for giving up a good job or for starting a business. But no one knows you as well as you. Trust what you know, and take action accordingly. The more you act on your instincts, the more instinctive you will become. Trusting my instincts led me to become the person I am today. Treat yourself with TLC. Seek to meet your mental, physical, spiritual and emotional needs by finding balance in all you do.

It's time to do that thing we all hate to do; look at ourselves in the mirror. We're really very good at a passing glance to make sure we don't have our makeup on wrong or our ties crooked or spinach in our teeth on our way out the door, but when was the last time you spent ten minutes just looking yourself in the eye?

In 1986, at the Whole Life Expo, there was a vendor there who had created a mirrored box you could sit in called a

"See". From your vantage point there were thousands of you from every angle possible to look. It was a very powerful meditation tool, to be sure. There was no hiding anything in there. It was distracting and focusing at the same time.

But to FOCUS, we need first to be clear about who we are and the goals we are pursuing

F: Fierce devotion to a goal.

O: Optimizing time, effort and resources

C: Creating new opportunities

U: Understanding what it is we want

S: Seeing the goal in 3D before it happens

Focus On Your Vision

Once we get back in touch with ourselves, it's time to get in touch with our vision. What was it that so enlivened you, lit you up and made you sparkle enough that you took the leap and created a business designed to make that vision a reality?

Can you write down your vision in 10 words or less so that someone else would "get it"? Why not take a few minutes to do so. If it's difficult to do, perhaps one of the things you've been lacking is F.O.C.U.S. Or perhaps you had it in the beginning and it's right there with the sticky notes under the business plan pieces, next to the receipts you have to enter into your accounting software.

F.O.C.U.S. is not only something we need as the word is defined, but it also is a check for our commitment to following our dream.

Let's take a closer look.

F: Fierce devotion to a goal

If our thoughts and hopes are elsewhere, it is impossible for us to set our faces steadily toward the work required of us.

◎ Anonymous

Fierce devotion to a goal is a difficult concept to explain. On the surface, it looks simple; it means to have that goal be your guiding force, the light you aim towards. However, it's a lot more than that. You have to be willing to make that goal the primary force in your life. You eat, sleep, breathe and live that goal every day. Nothing is more important than achieving it. The goal you set can be something apparently simple, but more often it's deeper, more expansive. A life where you are happy (however you define that), have what you require and more and the lifestyle that supports your choices is possibly more of a goal than a thriving business.

It's that unanswerable "why?" that fills you and drives you. Why do you want to do that thing you've envisioned. What was it that you want and why can't you get it any other way?

For me, it's wanting to make a difference in people's lives on a scale I cannot accomplish any other way.

I don't mean that there isn't anything else. You want the big "B", Balance, in your life, but somewhere in that creative genius you call a mind, there needs to be a compartment that is always on alert for opportunities to expand on your vision.

Your goals need to be SMART: Specific, Measurable, Attainable, Realistic and Time-Bound.

This means you have to be very SPECIFIC having the result you wish spelled out as well as the process. If you waffle on stating your goal, you'll waffle on getting it done.

When creating your goals, they need to be MEASURABLE, meaning there needs to be benchmarks and sub-goals along the way to evaluate progress.

Are they ATTAINABLE? Are they realistic with the resources and knowledge you have at hand right now or is there something else you need to acquire to achieve it?

Is your goal REALISTIC? Stretch yourself, but be clear. Brainstorm with a buddy – can what you want to do even be done in this physical reality?

And lastly, do you have a TIME for completion. Setting deadlines for decisions will help get them done as well as setting go/no go options.

Exercise 4   S.M.A.R.T. Goals

Identify a goal and see how it measures up by the S.M.A.R.T. Guidelines. You can do this for as many goals as you have.

Is it Specific? What is the desired result?

Is it Measurable? How will you measure progress and completion?

Is it Attainable? What skills are needed?

What resources are necessary? Are you prepared to make the commitments necessary in order to achieve it?

Is it Realistic? Brainstorm the goal, do not limit yourself, but seriously, can it be done?

Is it Time-Bound? What is the date by which you will accomplish the goal?

Your Goal Statement: (Begin goal statement with "I'm so happy and grateful now that..." state goal in present tense: "I am.." "I have...", etc. and must include date goal will be achieved).

O: Optimizing YOUR time and resources

Sleep is overrated. Sleep is for wimps. I'll sleep when I'm dead.

◉ Anonymous

We all have 24 hours in a day and 365 ¼ days in a year. Only 7 days in a week and there's a little flexibility where months are concerned, sort of. What we do with the time we have is not nearly as important as *how* we do it.

It's been said that entrepreneurs suffer from attention deficit disorders. We love to chase bright and shinies. Just when one idea is taking off, we'll veer off 180 degrees and chase off something else (or so it seems to the initiated, eh?)

To be fair, however, we do tend to be scattered in our attention. The discovery phase is always way more fun than the development and implementation phases.

So the big question is how do we use our time to the best advantage. When there's so much to do, how do we find some for ourselves, for our personal needs, without impacting anything else?

But it's not only limited to entrepreneurs. The syndrome also affects parents, teachers, students, people in relationships, ...

As I discuss later in the book, there are some creative ways to take time for you. Don't be afraid to be a little selfish. And schedule time for yourself the same way you would for a valued customer, project or event.

You are every bit as deserving of the attention. You can start small – 15 minutes with a timer. Just sit and listen to the ticking or play some music. But just take an uninterruptible 15 minutes only for you.

You'll be far better off for it.

C: Creating new opportunities

Opportunity is knocking; open the door!

◎ DeBorah Beatty

Stuff doesn't happen on its own. There is a serendipitous element to opportunity in its tendency to always be in motion. Opportunities are always flying by and if you don't capture them, the person standing behind you just might!

Here are a few tips for identifying/creating those fast-moving opportunities.

Stay alert and recognize patterns as they are forming. If your "spidey" sense starts tingling there's a good reason for it.

Look at the small things. Many of the best opportunities lie in what has been overlooked.

Don't overlook the obvious.

Watch for good ideas that are poorly executed.

Look for new, generally unknown information. If you can consolidate scattered ideas, you have an infoproduct (ebook, pamphlet or white paper).

Read journals, trade magazines, and online publications to keep on top of things and to gather new information that may inspire you.

Look for what has worked elsewhere. Be the first on your block. to ...

Look for new ways to meet old needs and wants.

Look for ways to overcome barriers that blocked a good idea in the past. Perhaps the barriers have lifted.

Look for "abandoned" markets

Look at why people buy something rather than what they buy.

Look for new uses for old products

Look for what's not working

Look for unhappy, dissatisfied people. They may point out needs and wants that you could fill.

Look for happy, contented people. These people will tell you what is working.

Always be observing, listening, waiting and thinking.. You never know where your next great idea will come from. And when you identify an opportunity, have a plan in mind for evaluation, development, implementation and exit. Will the opportunity be something you can take time right now to do or is it something you might want to sit on for a few months while you take care of what is on your desk today? Be smart about your time and your resources.

And remember, opportunity does not come in a single-serving container. Any good idea will usually spawn dozens of other ones.

U: Understanding what it is we want

If you want to make your dreams come true,

the first thing you have to do is wake up.

◉ J.M. Power

I don't know about you, but I've had a few occasions in my life where I thought I wanted something with all my heart and then when I got it, things just weren't what I thought they were going to be.

When we understand what it is we truly want, it's so much easier to go for them with focus and passion instead of getting misdirected by something we just have a passing fancy for.

Even better, however, is gaining clarity about whose desires they are! Are you trying to live for someone else who couldn't? Are you trying to be that xyz they never were? I know, especially among people my age, many of my generation were the first to go to college in the family and were living the dream for their parents who felt too old to do the same.

But how do you get in touch with what your deepest desire is? How do you weed out the distracting triple N's (Neat 'n' Nifties)? And moreover, how do we weed out what we tell ourselves we're supposed to want and separate that from that for which our heart truly yearns?

Recently I had a question on a product I had purchased. But after 15 minutes of being frustrated trying to explain what it was I was asking, I finally told the customer support person on the other end of the line what it was I wanted to do, why I wanted to do it and asked what I should ask if I want to do it again sometime.

Made me think. So many times, we're told to ask for what you want. The "Law of Attraction" tells us to concentrate on what we want to bring it to us. But the thing that is confounding most folks I speak with is how to be sure that what you're asking for is what you want.

One of the basic tenets of asking for what you want is being clear about the end result. Here's what I mean:

Close your eyes (well, AFTER you read this part) and imagine you're talking with your Faerie Godmother. She has in her hand a wand that will grant any one wish you have, but only one. What do you say to her, how do you phrase the question to be as precise as possible, given that this is something you have wanted forever and now have to figure out how to ask for it so you ensure you get it? Hard, isn't it?

So let's try a little trick of mine. Imagine you already have that which you crave the most; whatever that is. As I cover in my DreamBuilding 101 course, until you have a grasp on what it is you want that is solid enough to start seeing where it doesn't quite satisfy all your desires, it isn't real to you and remains at arms' length.

Getting really clear on the end result you desire from asking a question is a process just like anything else. I now use the following mental checklist when asking questions.

1. What do I want to do? (Desired result)

2. Why do I want to do it (Need)

3. What I've already done (Experience)

4. What is stopping me (Details)

5. Can I replicate it again with the information I receive?

My checklist has come in handy more often than I can tell you.

Perhaps the following exercise will help. It's part of my Disconnect Your Oughta Pilot™ system and has been very effective.

Exercise 4: Strengths, Passions & Obligations Assessment

Strengths Assessment:

What do you find were my greatest strengths?

What did I find were things I do well?

How do I best put my strengths to use?

What do others say are my strengths?

Passions Assessment:

What are the things you would like to do well?

What are the experiences you would like to have?

What do I want to start doing right now?

What are five nonnegotiable values in my life?

What things, events or activities make me feel fully alive?

What have I let slide? Why? What can I do now to reverse that?

What would be my "perfect day" at work? At home?

What would I do if I were guaranteed success in each of the various areas of life?

Write a paragraph describing your life if you were using all your talents and abilities?

Obligations Assessment

What is on your schedule that doesn't need to be there? What things can be abandoned or at least cut back? What obligations are you creating for six months from now that you might regret then?

Are any of the experiences that I would like to have that I have listed in my Passions Assessment reflected on my schedule? Weekly? Monthly? Yearly?

What are the things other people want you to do? What are the things YOU want to do?

What are some things you would like to do that fall under the category of "now or never"?

What is the 20 percent of your effort that produces 80 percent of the results you want to accomplish?

S: Seeing the goal before it happens

"The mind is the limit. As long as the mind can envision the fact that you can do something, you can do it, as long as you really believe 100 percent."

◉ Arnold Schwarzenegger

Have you ever seen something you dreamed of so clearly you could swear it was real? Have you ever wanted to go somewhere so strongly that you could close your eyes and be there? Could you smell the smells, taste the tastes, see the colors and the shadows in full 3D Dream-o-vision?

In my DreamBuilding 101 workshop, we go through several steps to clarify dreams to the level that they almost become memories and we know them so well, there's no way they can't happen.

Here's a brief overview of my process. You're welcome to try this yourself:

Step 1: Get in touch with the dream by getting quiet and then visualizing it in glorious, all enveloping detail.

Step 2: Discover what part of that dream you don't have a physical memory or image to match to it.

Step 3: Go find somewhere that you can create a physical experience of that part that's missing.

And then finally, come back to visualizing it and knowing that you now own it, see it microscopic detail.

Let's say one of the dreams you have is a new car. Get quiet and see yourself driving it. Sit quiet, mentally see yourself in the car, stretch your hands out and imagine how it will feel to grasp the steering wheel. Can you do it? Can you really really feel the car around you, smell the interior or feel the breeze from the air conditioner? Well, sort of.

Next, take yourself down to the dealership that sells those things. Go sit in the one you've been dreaming of. Now take a deep breath, smell the interior? Reach out your hands, grasp the steering wheel. How does it feel? Spongy?, hard, padded? How does your hind end feel in the seat? Your lower back?

Now that you know that, here's the fun part. What is wrong with the car? Are the drink holders in the wrong place for you? Hard to change the radio? Seat belts not where they need to be for your comfort?

You see, it's one of the perverse attributes of a human being that as long as something appears perfect and unattainable, all we can do is dream about it. Once we start finding things wrong with the thing we've dreamed of and longed for, it becomes much more real and reachable. It's almost like we only feel like we can't have something perfect. This bears further study and I'll report back as I figure things out.

Dreams are there to draw us forward, to strive towards a goal or make it through a challenge. We create them freely and often out of our dissatisfaction with what is and instead of changing what we can in the here and now, we put up and shut up and wait for someday.

But there is no someday. All we have is now. How many times have you seen people who spent their whole lives planning for that day when everything would be perfect and died before they could enjoy it? I sure don't want to be one of those people and I'm sure you don't either.

Live in the now. Create a vision. Live into that vision. Make it do-able, live-able, attainable and above all, enjoyable.

Part II: Re-Envision Your Life

Tips for a new perspective.

Ten Easy Steps

ONE: Commit To Beginning

"Start from where you are wherever that is"

Unknown

Any change can be intimidating. If you're feeling swallowed up in your business and don't feel like you have space to move and shift directions, you already recognize you need to change something somewhere.

The hardest part of any endeavor is beginning it. Lao Tzu is often quoted as having said, "A journey of a thousand miles begins with a single step." Although this is the popular form of this quotation, a more correct translation from the original Chinese would be "The journey of a thousand miles begins beneath one's feet." Rather than emphasizing the first step, Lau Tzu regarded action as something that arises naturally from stillness.

How many people talk about doing something but talking is all they do? It is possible to talk a dream to death. You can also plan a dream to death.

You can spend so much time planning or "getting it right", you never begin; or you can wait so long, what you want to do to take advantage of a cutting edge opportunity doesn't work anymore and in fact, that cutting edge is now old news!

I see this all the time in friends, colleagues, and the forums I follow. The thought of not doing something just the right way (whatever that means to the individual) is so paralyzing, so intimidating, they are rooted where they stand and can't think of what to do first. I have attempted, I have failed, I survived. This is part of what I talk about in my Joys of Failure program.

<u>If you've never done a certain thing before, you have nothing to compare the result to and _you_ are the only one who can decide whether you've failed at all!</u>

Failure is all in YOUR mind. How many people do you know that blow off compliments saying that they could have done better and then list excuses? Especially when they've done something you've been trying to do and have been unable to succeed?

There comes a time to decide whether to let a failure (which I define as not achieving a goal you set) stop you cold or offer you a springboard to a better, more strategic attempt.

Think of a skateboarder going over a speedbump. If they hit the speedbump in just the right way, they'll splat themselves on the asphalt. But if they approach it another way, they grab air and soar.

The way I begin is to end; that is, I start at the desired result and work back to the very beginning spark of inspiration. That way you see the progression and the causal relationships in each step.

You can set achievable benchmarks and quantify your measures to determine how successful each milestone is. I know that sounds a little intense, but it's actually much easier to know where you're heading than to just blindly stomp through the wastelands hoping for a path to reveal itself to you.

In a metaphysical sense, by committing to beginning, you start the forward movement of the energy that will bring that dream to fruition. That's why I say to planifest your visions and dreams.

Nike's "Just Do It" campaign became legendary and made the company millions while lifting it out of a tough time against Reebok. The paper by the CFAR (Center For Applied Research) is an inspiring read. It's available online at http://www.cfar.com/Documents/nikecmp.pdf.

TWO: Take A Look Around

How you do what you do and do you feel you do well at it? Do you want to shave a few minutes here and there to have some personal time?

You can't trim until you know how you do something and can see where there might be extra steps in the process.

You know what you do; you know how to do it quite well. Or, at least you think you do.

Identify what is working and what is not.

When was the last time you actually tracked a process from beginning to end to see where the trim spots were? It's actually a very good exercise to track your processes and write them down.

In business we have Operations Manuals or Policies and Procedures manuals. These say who does what, where and for how much. You can do the same thing for yourself.

Make a personal operations manual and journal all the things you accomplish in a day. At the end of your exercise, just sit a moment and take it in. My goodness, you are a wonder!

Enjoy that accomplishment before you move on to the next activity. Own that you are capable and efficient.

If there were places where you felt you did less than what you could have done or took a shortcut, own that, too.

Until you accept your life as it is, and take control, you will have a difficult time changing anything that isn't working.

When things go other than the way we plan, we've very conscious of the disconnect and quite often have a lot to say about it. I think it's because when things work well, they are transparent and don't require attention so we often miss them entirely.

So first, let's look at how you begin to track what's working then we'll move on to what is not.

You're going to need some paper and something to write with for this next part.

What works:

Let's begin with something simple. What is something that you get compliments on? Let' say for the sake of this process that people compliment you on how cheerful you always sound when you answer the phone.

Close your eyes. Imagine the phone ringing. What do you do first? Do you just grab it and say hello? Or is there something you say or do when you answer the phone to get ready? Whichever way you do it, write it down. Begin with the phone ringing.

Here's a sample scenario:

Phone rings.

You pick up the receiver and smile.

You answer with however you answer – write it down if you use the same phrase.

You begin speaking with the person on the other end of the phone. You answer their questions, address their issue or whatever else is needed.

The conversation ends.

So? Now what? Do you do anything else? Do you make a note? Anything you do before, during or after answering and having the conversation needs to be documented.

Do this for all the other events in your day. Take as long as you want. I usually recommend doing this process for 7 days so you get a real feel for what your activities truly are.

Also keep in mind how you feel when you do these activities. What part of a process do you enjoy, what part makes you cringe. Write that down, too.

THREE: Evaluate

Now that you have the last task complete, what did it show you? Do you have a happy life or is there something that needs changing?

As human beings, we have a huge tolerance for mediocre. We tolerate rather than change. I'm the same way and totally not immune. We'll put up with status quo for years even though it makes us crazy. What are you tolerating? What compromises have you made unconsciously?

There's nothing wrong with compromise. Let me address this here. Compromise is a mature, effective way to handle situations that would otherwise be intolerable.

When you are faced with a request, do you think you only have two options? Do you say yes or no? There is a third option and that is to negotiate or modify the request so that both parties get what they need.

In successful negotiations, one thing to remember is that both parties need to win. Compromise and negotiating are not supposed to be tools to a solution that have a clear winner and loser. These are two tools that are designed to have the teeter-totter be level with both sides even at the end.

What gets you off track? How are you distracted from what you need to do? Are you plagued by hundreds of emails popping into view on your computer or phone? Is it phone calls interrupting your meetings? Or is it just a few levels of Bejeweled or that solitaire game between tasks? Whatever the "it" is, it's keeping you from being productive, getting finished with your projects and having the time to create more. And I'm not just talking about business tasks here.

Once I did this same exercise, I found that if I tweaked one thing I could save two hours a day! What I did was to create a habit of checking my email at 10am and 3pm and other than that, I did not have it running. That way I was not enticed by a popup telling me I had mail and distracting me until I went to see if something important needed my attention.

Another thing I did was to turn off all social networking notifications. All those notices from Facebook and Linked In clamoring for my attention were nothing more than interrupters. In the time it took to stop what I was doing, and go to see what was going on, I lost my train of thought and often couldn't get back to it after finding out that all the person sending me the notice wanted was to play a game! What I do now is schedule Social Network time every day to check my inbox, reply to anything that needs it, read new posts in my groups and make comments and I'm done in 30 to 45 minutes.

This includes text messages and emails on my phone. Anyone who knows my ID to text me knows I won't answer between the hours of 8 and 5 unless it's an emergency (and we all have a code for that). I suggest something like that for you, as well.

Anything that distracts you from your task at hand is a timewaster. It can be the phone, email, kids, pets – the list goes on.

I'm not saying not to pay attention to your kids, phone, pets, etc. But wherever possible, keep to a schedule.

FOUR: Automate Repetitive Tasks

How many times do you do the same thing over and over again? Isn't that monotonous?

Is there any part of any task that could be automated or shortened? Short of outsourcing (which is another topic), there are numerous ways to figure out what parts of what we do can be automated or shortened. I'm not talking about robotics, just using tools to their best advantage. Here's a good example:

Instead of responding to every email request as they come in, group them together. Set aside a time every day to do email tasks.

Is there a task you do so often there's no thought involved anymore? Is there a way to shortcut any of the steps? Write every step down. Years ago when I worked at Intel, they sent us through training to write what they called "Breathe In, Breathe Out Specifications". Do you know there are 39 steps to writing a note to someone? Seriously! Do you have to send out the same packet of information all the time? Do you have those packets bundled and ready in envelopes to just be addressed when the call comes in? Or, when it comes to requests for brochures, do you have envelopes prestuffed with the brochures and your business card just waiting to be addressed and mailed? These are the kinds of things you can delegate or do yourself while watching a movie at home.

Once you start thinking through ways to save yourself time and shortcut/automate the repetitive tasks, it really becomes much easier to find the shortcuts.

FIVE: Create and Use A Personal Operations Manual

What would happen if you weren't available sometime? What if you got sick or had to have surgery or what if you went to visit Great Aunt Sally? Would your company, family, or life continue nicely without you or would it fall apart?

How much time is spent trying to remember a small detail when opportunities arise? When you're the chief cook and bottle washer and do everything, it's difficult to remember every little detail. If something worked really well, we tend to like to repeat the process, but if it takes you longer to remember it than to do it, you don't gain anything. Even Albert Einstein said he never remembered anything he could write down. I think I'd like to be in his league.

If you wanted to outsource some of your work to a friend to help with the overwhelm, would you be able to tell them how to handle situations or issues the same way you would and could you give them guidelines to do so?

Here are some of the things Operations Manuals can do for you:

- Keep track of where things are and who to call for what and when

- Keep copies of important documentation; i.e., warranties, contracts, lists of babysitters, agencies, daycare facilities, addresses of friends and family, etc.

- Have the instructions for reprogramming the microwave or new fandangled coffeemaker so you can find them easily.

In business, these documents are useful for marketing and managing day to day operations. In your daily life, you're CEO at You, Inc. and have somewhat the same types of responsibilities. You may not have the collateral samples (brochures, business cards, graphics for corporate ID, etc.) but you still have enough stuff to keep track of that it warrants a central place to do it in.

It doesn't have to be formidable or even formal. It can be a collection of sticky notes for all it matters; just some way to write down what you do and how you do it.

Personally, I like to use a 3-ring binder with sheet protectors so I can slide things in whenever I come up with something. (After all, when you print things out, they're normally on 8 ½ x 11 inch paper anyway, right?) I just print an extra copy of everything I use often. The next time you come to one of my events, ask me to show my ops manual to you. I always have it with me to refer to – ESPECIALLY IF I HAVE TO BE

OUT OF TOWN. That way, if I need a copy of a license, insurance policy or anything else, I have it ready to provide.

I've also seen collections of index cards (like in a recipe box), a single spiral notebook or if you like to have fun with things the way I do, a most assuredly juvenile binder with stickers and sparkles all over it. (Yes, I had a Strawberry Shortcake Trapper Keeper for awhile that "graduated" to a My Pretty Pony one later. Hey, I liked the glitter, what can I say?) I'm not even sure if they still make Trapper Keepers but they were wonderful for this.

Your operations manual should be your best friend. Why spend the time and energy trying to remember the small details when you can write them down when you come up with them and just refer to them later.

The book is also a wonderful place to keep an Idea Journal for those stray bright and shinies that encroach on your day and distract you from what you're doing. If you get them written down, once your day is complete and you have all your tasks done, you can play a little and revisit them. (Not only that, but sometimes, just by letting them sit quietly waiting for you, the ideas that are not worthy of a second look take care of themselves, if you know what I mean.)

Here's a list of what I recommend you include in your Personal Operations Manual:

- Process notes (how you do what you do and when to do it)

- List of contacts in case your regular support is unavailable (babysitters, daycare, doctors, cab companies, mechanics)

- Any forms you use for any reason

- List of contacts in case you can't function (attorney, accountant, doctors, family, etc.)

- Spiral notebook for ideas

The list above is only a bare bones starter to get you thinking. I'm sure you'll think of other things as you go along.

This is an especially good habit to get into. Many times when you're faced with a challenge, the last thing you can remember is where some paperwork is that you need.

I've even know a gal who kept current school pictures of her kids in hers so that if anything ever happened to any of them, she'd have a current picture to provide to authorities. She kept current pictures of her husband and herself in there, too.

It also works well if you're a busy person with community activities. If you've created a flier that worked well for a fundraiser, you can keep a copy for the next time something comes up.

NOTES:

_____
_____
_____
_____
_____
_____
_____
_____
_____
_____
_____
_____
_____
_____

SIX: Seek Out And Create Partnerships Of Excellence

I am an only child. I am a solopreneur, I do a lot of my work alone. Well, sort of. You see, I have built Partnerships of Excellence to help me out.

Partnerships of Excellence are a wonderful to share the load and ease the frustrations of too much to do too often.

What are these Partnerships of Excellence and how do they happen? I define PE's as relationships where others who do what I do not do well out of natural ability and love of the task working with me in a relationship for mutual gain.

Loosely translated that means I find people who love doing the things I'm less than effective doing (or hate doing, to be perfectly honest with you), create a relationship with them and entering into a partnership where my skills help them and their skills help me.

I'm sure you know what I'm talking about – you have those people who are amazing at writing and do it as effortlessly as breathing. Yet the writers can't balance their checkbooks to save their lives. Ideally, they would go in search of people who love the satisfaction of balancing checkbooks

127

and don't give it a second glance since it's so easy for them, but can't write a sentence that makes sense for their newsletter.

These two connect to create a Partnership of Excellence and both win — the writer writes and the checkbook balancer balances checkbooks. Both are happy and both are much more effective because they're doing what they love and what is natural for them instead of agonizing and pushing to complete tasks they hate and which take twice as long because they're so downright difficult and repugnant.

Think of this in a relationship – if you are the one in the couple who loves to cook, records hours of The Food Network for your day off, and writes up menus in your sleep, then you do that part.

If, on the other hand, you are the one in the relationship who can't boil water without burning it, and your significant other is a whiz at preparing tasty meals but can't pick up after themselves to save their lives and you are a compulsive neatnik, you let them do the cooking and you clean.

Partnerships of Excellence. They work.

In business, these partnerships are critical. You cannot and need not be expected to do everything well. Why waste your time doing what frustrates you and stresses you out? In daily life, how many times have young mothers found partnerships for childcare, play groups, shopping, sharing groceries from Costco, etc. Don't you have tasks you just HATE to do?

Of course you do.

Finding others who enjoy doing those same nasty tasks and offering to do the things they hate to do, providing you're better at them, is just good sense. All it takes is a conversation to find out where assistance is needed.

Take inventory of what needs to be done, look around at the next networking event you attend and see if there is someone there who needs what you do well and does what you don't or can't. See if the chemistry works between the two of you and there you are on your way to a Partnership of Excellence. Easy breezy.

SEVEN: Create and Honor Sacred Space/Time

Even Superman had his sanctum sanctorum, his Fortress of Solitude, where he could get away from all the people who needed him and rest, recover or just have peace and quiet for a change.

Do you have a place of your own to think, meditate, plan and dream? If you do, good for you. If you don't, why not? And, more importantly, if you have one, do you use it?

When you don't have a place that is yours alone, kids-free, spouse-free, business-free and inviolate, it's rather like trying to get a good night's sleep in the middle of the freeway!

We all need a sacred space to recharge our batteries; particularly when you're running a business that has you pulled in several directions at once.

So what is sacred space, exactly?

Sacred space will mean different things to different people, but in its barest form, it means a space where you can be undisturbed, at peace and relaxed. A place you can leave stress outside of and others respect. It can even be a virtual space like a fairy garden in a potted plant that you can mentally visit to refresh yourself.

It can be as simple as a favorite chair where you can enjoy a cup of your favorite beverage or an actual room set aside for meditation or yoga or whatever recharges and refreshes you.

Depending on your own beliefs and practices, your space can be whatever you choose. I have clients who use their designated sacred space for reading and reflecting on Bible passages first thing in the morning and for taking a 15-minute break mid afternoon to catch their breath. I have friends who have a designated sacred space for doing yoga, meditating and their morning and evening prayers. Another friend of mine considers her bathtub sacred space. So it's most definitely what you choose it to be.

I first read about creating a sacred space several years ago in Sarah Ban Breathnach's beautiful book "Simple Abundance." I felt like I needed a place to calm myself, and recharge on a regular basis. My world was crashing around my ears and I wanted to remove myself from the drama and recharge.

I like to come into my own space, take a few deep breaths, light a small candle and just be still to see what the Universe has to share with me. It's usually some wonderfulness that I missed while tearing around being busy.

Setting up a Sacred Space is different in your home and at an office, too, obviously. I suggest the following

For someone working at home:

Find a corner with good energy. It can be anywhere, actually.

Go "shopping". Look around your home and find something that elicits a strong response in you — a painting, a statue, even a piece of fabric that has meaning for you.

Set up some way of identifying that space as yours – a small table as an altar, a shelf, a chair and throw.

Ask yourself what you need to add to the space and listen to your Inner Self for the answer. You know what you've been missing.

Set aside a time each day to occupy that space, add soft, soothing music on an MP3 player. Spend at least 15 minutes allowing a conversation with the Universe and clearing your mind.

For someone working externally:

Find a space where you can be undisturbed. If you have a door you can close, your whole office can be Sacred Space.

Bring in a few things that will call to you to spend quiet time with them. An item to put on your bookshelf that has a special meaning is good, or a piece of artwork you can get lost in for a few moments a day. It's about feeling you're worth spending the time on and *YOU ARE!*

Set aside a time every day to occupy that space, add soft, soothing music on an MP3 player. Spend at least 15 minutes allowing a conversation with the Universe and clearing your mind. Send your mind out to play and see what it comes home with – you will be surprised!

Space is not the only thing you need to hold sacred.

There is also time. How many times do you blow off spending quiet time or doing something you were looking forward to because you have just "one more thing" to get out of the way before you go. Ever have that one more thing turn into ten? Me, too.

When you set up your own appointments you wouldn't think of not keeping them would you? Your dentist will charge your for a no show as might a hairdresser or client. Well, how about making an appointment with yourself every day or every few days to check in and see how things are going? AND KEEP THAT APPOINTMENT!

We tend to minimize the importance of "Me Time". I know, it seems to be a luxury to look forward to rather than experience. I used to feel the same way. But what needs to happen here is a shift to feeling that we are as important as those people we are scheduling time with. We are. After all, without us they would not have their business, right?

How about trying this one on during the next few days:

As CEO of You, Inc., take your company star employee (yourself) out to lunch or dinner.

Spend time with them and get to know what makes them happy, what their dreams are and how they fit into your business plan.

You'd do it in a heartbeat if you had an employee who gave countless hours of their own time, were dedicated to your vision and making the business work, wouldn't you? Would you skip the appointment if you knew how much it would mean to your employee?

If the shoe were on the other foot, would you skip the appointment if your CEO were asking you out to lunch specifically? Heck no. So, take yourself out to lunch or dinner and spend a little time with you. Make sure you keep that time sacred.

Set yourself some limits. Decide what time you want to start and what time you want to finish. You're the boss, after all. Then do so. Honor that commitment to yourself and your life. The things you'd be working on will be there tomorrow and I promise you, with 99% of the tasks on your desk, they'll wait and you'll be far more effective for having honored your agreement with yourself and gotten a good rest before tackling them.

Write down a few commitments you want to make to yourself on the next page. Have fun with it.

NOTES:

EIGHT: Spend More Time Being Selfish

Be selfish. You're the only YOU you've got!

Learn to say "no" occasionally. I know, I know. We have a difficult time saying the "n" word. We think it will make others think less of us and we so desperately care what they think.

We've all been taught that being selfish is a bad thing. I agree that putting your desires always before anyone else's or always acting on your own behalf is not a good thing, but when the other side of that is forsaking all self care and nurturing is also not good. There needs to be a balance. There is really no reward for self-sacrifice.

There is a good selfishness and a bad selfishness with the poles at opposite ends of the spectrum. Bad selfishness is what all the dictionaries define – thinking of self ahead of everything else and not caring about anyone or anything else. Good selfishness, as I see it, is realizing that as an individual we are part of a community and that the community contributes to us on levels we are unaware of.

Individuals are a microcosm (a Western philosophical term designating man as being a "little world" in which the macrocosm, or universe, is reflected - per Encyclopedia Brittanica). Being focused on managing and nurturing our selves ultimately is contributing back to the community of which we are a part.

Try to think of it this way: if you don't take care of yourself, there won't be anyone to take care of your family, your friends, etc. If you've flown recently, the flight attendants will remind that in case of an emergency requiring the oxygen mask, to take care of yourself first before helping anyone else.

If an opportunity comes by and it doesn't further what you have set as your focus, let it go on by! It's okay. Because if you let it go and stay available to those things that do forward your focus, those opportunities will come rushing in to take its place soon enough. Opportunities fly by at an amazing rate. If you focus on what is before you and truly examine and commit to where you're going, you'll see them suddenly seem to multiply. They've always been there, but you were distracted chasing the other things.

The easiest place to start saying no is with email. Don't subscribe to every newsletter that *might* have something to do with what you're doing. If they don't serve you, unsubscribe and let go. They only distract you from what you're doing now.

Next is your phone. Do you get a lot of phone calls or text messages? Are they really important when they interrupt you from what you're doing? Do you ever turn the phone off when you're writing or working on a specific project? (You can, you know.) Then designate a time to return all your calls. Notify your friends, family, customers or clients and everyone who needs to know that you have a new policy going into place to maximize your effectiveness. Tell them what time is good to reach you and only take calls during that time. It will be hard at first, but it does work to improve efficiency and productivity.

NOTES:

Nine: Do A Little DreamBuilding

How do you know you have what you want if you don't know what it feels like? As human beings we are endowed with five senses: sight, hearing, smell, touch, and taste. Some are endowed with more. Edwin P. Hubble says we have seven; the five mentioned above as well as intuition and equilibrium.

I mention these because it takes all of them to create what I call a *concrete imagining*. As I mentioned earlier, when DreamBuilding, it's critical to use all the senses. See the dream, smell it, listen for all the noises that are there, taste it, have it consume your awareness. When someone mentions a fresh, ripe strawberry, you can easily smell it, taste it and see it, can't you? DreamBuilding is the process to get what you're dreaming of be present in the same vivid level.

There are a few steps involved that can be rather fun, actually. The first one is to **see** what you want before you in every teensy, tiny detail. If it helps to close your physical eyes and open your imagining ones, do that. What? You didn't know you had another set of handy dandy envisioners? Well you do. Deep inside your mind. They're part of your pre-installed make believe system you developed as a child. You have an entire set of sensory input devices there you can access just for imagining.

What colors are there in the thing you want? What shape is it? How big is it in reference to something else you can relate to? From a sight standpoint only, what is the texture of the surface? (We'll get to what it feels like in a minute). How do you think it would feel?

Next, close your mental eyes that you are looking at your dream with. Take a deep breath. Can you smell anything? If so, can you identify the scent? If you can't place it, what does it remind you of? Can you see that other thing, too?

Depending on what the vision/dream thing is, can you taste it? Does it have taste? If it's a physical thing like a car or a house, is there a metallic taste or a taste in the back of your throat from something growing near it?

Is the thing you are envisioning have a sound? Is it you in front of an audience? Are they laughing, clapping, cheering or just sitting quietly and all you hear is the sound of paper and pencils busily taking down your every word while others squeak in their chairs as they get more comfortable or reach for something.

I think you can tell where this is going. Take each sense individually and maximize the sensory awareness of the thing you are working to create. Then, (and this is the really interesting part of this whole pursuit), when you can see it, and feel it, smell it and taste it. When it is so real you have no doubt when you open your physical eyes it will be before you, take a moment and think about what's missing with it. What could it be to make it even better?

It's part of human perversity that while imagining a thing, no matter how clearly, we hold it "out there" at arm's reach. Just beyond our fingertips, we strain to grab on to it and possess it. Once we can see it so clearly we can start finding fault with it, the thing that has eluded us moves into our range and we can now make it real.

Think about it. Whenever you've attempted to imagine something to attract it, how successful have you been when it became your holy grail, something to seek? Putting it on a vision board, mindmapping it, using all the tools there are to envision a thing you want only served to keep it close. But still it eluded your grasp.

When you start seeing it so clearly that it's minor defects appear, you have truly envisioned so clearly, so thoroughly, that you will, in fact, bring it to yourselves.

Ten: Where Do We Go From Here?

To recap, we've discussed the parts to my Disconnect Your Oughta Pilot™ Program. It requires you being present to who you are as a person, acknowledging your needs and honoring them while keeping all the other parts of your life in perspective.

As a third-generation entrepreneur, I am intimately familiar with the challenges of having a life and a business. As a single mother I was acutely familiar with the challenges of being a parent as well as a person.

I know what it takes to drive towards a goal, but I also know burnout at the other end won't let you enjoy it when you get there (if you even can recognize the success when it comes, that is.)

Going through all the stages I've described previously saved my sanity, restored my feelings of self-worth and created the life I now lead. I want these things for you as well. I know what's possible even though life appears uncertain and you feel powerless to change anything. I know what it feels like to be immobilized by fear or reluctant to rock the boat. Believe me, I've been there at one point (and in some cases many points) in my life. The one thing that got me through all of it was the belief that in spite of what everyone else thought, I was worth something and I have something to contribute.

If ever I can be of further assistance to you, either in one of my Living In Left Field Action Groups or in a one-on-one mentoring/coaching relationship, please contact me. I'd love to hear from you.

I've included information on my programs in Appendix A in the Resources Section, next.

PART III: Resources

Appendix A:

Working Dictionary

Dream   Something untenable, without form, a vague wish or hope for someday

Vision   A driving force leading you forward to do, be or have something more than you currently perceive in your reality. A knowing inside of your passions, abilities and strengths and how they need to be committed to the future.

Planifesting   The process of working backwards from a fulfilled vision, establishing benchmarks, dreambuilding, enrolling your community and mastering your environment.

DreamBuilding   A way to create the experience of having what you envision right here, right now, wherever you are in the process of planifesting your future.

Oughta Pilot™   Giving up what you know is right for you to follow what others say you "oughta" do, denying the   skills you were born with in favor of those you've learned along the way

Original Song   Skills you were born with and are such a part of you as to be invisible. These are the abilities you have that lets you do some tasks as naturally as breathing.

Concrete Imagining   A method of using all the senses to create a vision for action. Part of DreamBuilding.

Failure   Not achieving a goal.

Reality vs reality   "Big R reality" is unchangeable, unmutable as in being held to the planet by something called gravity or the notion that water is wet and rocks are hard (although those are language constructs as well but that's for another book). "Little r reality" is the concept of reality we create for ourselves and take as true, but may not necessarily be so; i.e., "I can't catch a break", "life is difficult and requires a struggle", etc.

This is an excellent daily exercise to assist with self-esteem. Make a commitment to yourself every day.

My Personal Commitment

I, _____, am serious about setting and reaching my goals in my life, so on this _____day of _____, 20_____, I promise myself that I will take the first step toward setting those goals.

I am willing to exchange temporary pleasures in the pursuit of happiness and the striving for excellence in the pursuit of my goals. I am willing to discipline my physical and emotional appetites to reach the long-range goals of happiness and accomplishment. I recognize that to reach my goals I must grow personally and have the right mental attitude, so I promise to specifically increase my knowledge in my chosen field and regularly read positive growth books and magazines. I will also attend lectures and seminars, take courses in personal growth and development. I will utilize my time more effectively by enrolling in the University on Wheels and listening to motivational and educational recordings while driving or performing routine tasks at home or in the yard. I will keep a list of my activities including the completion dates for each project in my Goals Program. I further promise to list good ideas (mine and those of others) and to note thoughts, power-phrases, and quotations which have meaning to me.

Better Than Good

Affirmations for daily living by Zig Ziglar

From <u>Better Than Good</u> ©2006 Reprinted with permission.

1. I am doing better than good because I clearly understand that failure is an event; not a person, that yesterday ended last night and today is my brand new day.

2. I am doing better than good because I have made friends with my past, am focused on the present, and optimistic about my future.

3. I am doing better than good because I know that success (a win) doesn't make me and failure (a loss) doesn't break me.

4. I am doing better than good because I am filled with faith, hope and love and live without anger, greed, built, envy or thoughts of revenge.

5. I am doing better than good because I am mature enough to delay gratification and shift my focus from my rights to my responsibilities.

6. I am doing better than good because I know that failure to stand for what is morally right is the prelude to being the victim of what is criminally wrong.

7. I am doing better than good because I am secure in who I am, so I am at peace and in fellowship with all people.

8. I am doing better than good because I have made friends of my adversaries, and have gained the love and respect of those who know me best.

9. I am doing better than good because I understand that others can give me pleasure, but genuine happiness comes from when I do things for others.

10. I am doing better than good because I am pleasant to the grouch, courteous to the rude, and generous to the needy.

11. I am doing better than good because I love the unlovable, give hope to the hopeless, friendship to the friendless and encouragement to the discouraged.

12. I am doing better than good because I can look back in forgiveness, forward in hope, down in compassion and up with gratitude.

13. I am doing better than good because I recognize, confess, develop and use my Spirit-given

physical, mental and spiritual abilities for the benefit of mankind.

14. Add some of your own:

AFFIRMATIONS:

_____

_____

_____

_____

_____

_____

_____

_____

_____

_____

_____

_____

_____

The Butterfly

Author: Unknown

A man found a cocoon for a butterfly. One day a small opening appeared, he sat and watched the butterfly for several hours as it struggled to force its body through the little hole.

Then it seemed to stop making any progress. It appeared as if it had gotten as far as it could and could go no farther. Then the man decided to help the butterfly.

He took a pair of scissors and snipped the remaining bit of the cocoon. The butterfly then emerged easily.

Something was strange. The butterfly had a swollen body and shriveled wings. The man continued to watch the butterfly because he expected at any moment, the wings would enlarge and expand to be able to support the body, which would contract in time.

Neither happened. In fact, the butterfly spent the rest of its life crawling around with a swollen body and deformed wings. It was never able to fly.

What the man in his kindness and haste did not understand, was that the restricting cocoon and the struggle required for the butterfly to get through the small opening of the cocoon are God's way of forcing fluid from the body of the butterfly into its wings so that it would be ready for flight once it achieved its freedom from the cocoon.

Sometimes struggles are exactly what we need in our life. If God allowed us to go through all our life without any obstacles, that would cripple us. We would not be as strong as what we could have been.

Not only that, we could never fly.

What's Next?

If you always do what you've always done
you will always get what you always got.

◉ Henry Ford

Living In Left Field Action Group: This program was designed with one very clear goal in mind... to help people just like you achieve a thriving, joyful, way of living a life of your own creation. I have groups focused on business, relationships and personal goals.

We're talking about a quantum leap in the direction of your dreams!

If you're serious about making a change in the way your life happens, then you've got to get in on this! Where else can you get this sort of attention?

There are a lot of great tools out there for helping keep your Big Picture goals clearly in mind. But that's nothing compared to the power of a Mastermind or having a really focused, knowledgeable coach like me that will keep you on track AND show you how to implement those bright and brilliant ideas you've been having.

A Mastermind is a group of committed entrepreneurs with the power to break through barriers and unlock opportunities you didn't even know were there. When you also have a facilitator in the group who can lead you in the right direction, it's powerful.

In a Mastermind or group mentoring program, all of a sudden, ideas are flying; breakthroughs are happening left and right, and suddenly, you've got a crystal clear picture of what needs to happen in order for you to reach your goals.

What You Get: The focus of this 6-week group coaching program is on getting each and every participant on the road to clarity, a re-emergence of passion and presence to possibility — and I can't wait for you to see the kind of results this group is going to produce!

The business-oriented sessions focus on creating a lifestyle-oriented business; one where you call the shots — where you have the systems and support in place to make money while maintaining your chosen quality of life. It's what everybody wants, but very few know how to create (or take the time to create). If you're serious about your financial goals AND your freedom — and are ready for a real breakthrough — then I cannot emphasize strongly enough, you've got to get in on this program!

Not only will you have access to a mastermind group of six other entrepreneurs as passionate about their success as you are, but you'll learn my PROVEN Living in Left Field System and lifestyle oriented business techniques AND have access to personalized coaching each and every week!

The artist-oriented sessions focus on creating with no expectation of perfection – just creating. We'll do a creativity exercise at the beginning of each session, then each participant will be given an opportunity to share anything they feel moved to share – breakthroughs, new projects, frustrations, anything that they want support with from the rest of the group.

I'm also planning a breakthrough group for couples, for parents, for parents and teens and for teens. Sign up on my website to keep up to date with the groups forming.

So, if you're ready to dramatically accelerate your progress — and get a jump on the life you want to live — you owe it to yourself to take action now and reserve your spot in this powerful new program!

What It Costs: For only $99 per 6-week session, you get the above PLUS downloadable recordings of all the sessions, unedited so you can be present again to the magic of each session.

Disconnect Your Oughta Pilot™ Modules:

These are one-on-one modular programs that can be taken individually or in a progression that builds upon each prior course. They include:

Disconnecting Your Oughta Pilot™

- Discovering Your Original Song

- Walking Your Talk

- Planifesting Your Future

- Purpose/Creativity

- Time Management

There are also modular programs that include:

- Business Evaluation

- Creating An Operations Manual

About DeBorah Beatty

I teach people who have put their lives and dreams on hold how to re-envision their lives, disconnect their Oughta Pilots™ and live their purpose — on their terms — with power, passion and possibility.

A Woman of Diverse Talents

As a mentor,DeBorah brings 50 years of business experience as well as a lifetime of recovering from adversity, refusing to be stopped from living her dream, a created life.

As a speaker and workshop leader, her signature "Disconnect Your Oughta Pilot(tm)" program is quickly becoming a crowd favorite whenever the 1-day intensives are offered.*

As an author, DeBorah's books and CDs allow her public to take a little bit of her with them wherever they go.

*If you would like to request a workshop in your area, please contact us.

Teaching You To Live Your *Own* Life

DeBorah has spent her life in the School of Hard Knocks and has graduated Suma Cum Laude! Her Disconnect Your Oughta Pilot^{TM} and Living A Created Life programs are becoming a standard for those who wish to reclaim control of their lives and manifest their visions. She's survived disasters of varying kinds and has found her way back after losing everything several times. She knows what it takes to pick herself up and keep going.

She will:

- Help you rediscover your Original Song (natural skills you were born with)
- Provide measurable benchmarks for success in new endeavors
- Identify alternatives to doing things yourself
- Provide resources and networks for support

- Provide ongoing coaching to ensure new systems and processes continue to run smoothly

About Created Life Strategies

CREATED LIFE STRATEGIES is committed to helping those who come to us to choose and live a created life of joy, of adventure and fun. We want you to experience a renewed zest and delight in a life full of power, passion and possibility where you are in charge of your own path, armed with tools and support to go forward and recognize yourself as the amazing phenomenon we see you to be.

We provide the tools and ongoing support to our graduates. Workshops, focus groups, group and one-on-one coaching are all part of the programs we offer.

We offer a complimentary 30-minute, get acquainted session so you can see if we're what you're looking for.

For more information on these and other programs, contact us at contact@createdlife.com.

About Created Life Publishing And This Book

CREATED LIFE PUBLISHING is a wholly owned subsidiary of Created Life Strategies. We are dedicated to offering quality work that furthers the goal of our readers to live a created life.

Disconnect Your Oughta Pilot is the first in a series scheduled for release through 2013. Watch for our next book, Disconnect Your Oughta Pilot for Solopreneurs scheduled for November 2012 publication.

Another fine product from Created Life Publishing:

How do you attract what you want?

Hoping and wishing don't work. Here's a tool that will get you in action and moving towards your dreams.

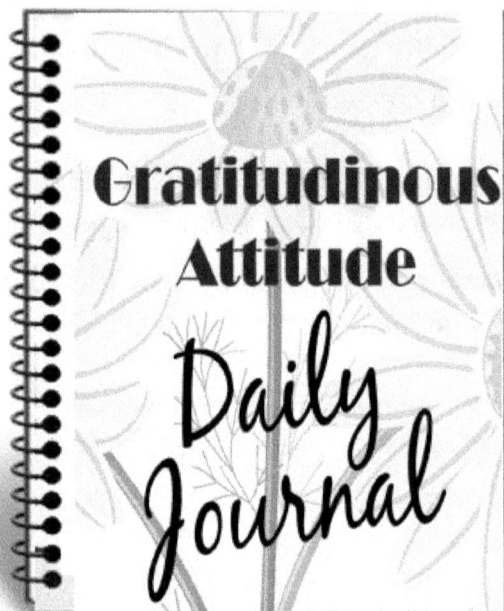

Order your copy today. Only $19.95

Available from Created Life Publishing

http://createdlife.com/products/books/

Thank you for purchasing and reading this book. You've taken a step on your journey and I support you 100% in your endeavors.

Now, go out and live YOUR created life.

www.ingramcontent.com/pod-product-compliance
Lightning Source LLC
LaVergne TN
LVHW021449080426
835509LV00018B/2220